Sales and Operations for Your Small Business

Sales and Operations for Your Small Business

E. JAMES BURTON
STEVEN M. BRAGG

WILEY
John Wiley & Sons, Inc.
New York • Chichester • Weinheim • Brisbane • Singapore • Toronto

Library of Congress Cataloging-in-Publication Data:

Burton, E. James
    Sales and operations for your small business / E. James Burton, Steven M. Bragg.
      p. cm.
    Includes index.
    ISBN 0-471-39704-0 (pbk. : alk. paper)
    1. Sales management. 2. Small business—Management. I. Bragg, Steven M. II. Title.

HF5438.4.B87 2000
658.8'1—dc21
                                            00-039238

About the Authors

E. James Burton, Ph.D., CPA, CFE, is dean of the College of Business and a full professor of accounting at Middle Tennessee State University. He has founded, owned, managed, and sold a number of businesses in a variety of areas from service to manufacturing. He received a Bachelor of Arts degree from MacMurray College in economics/business, a Master of Business Administration degree from Murray State University in management, and a Ph.D. in accountancy from the University of Illinois at Urbana-Champaign. In addition to over 50 journal articles, he has written *Total Business Planning: A Step-by-Step Guide with Forms* that has continued through three editions and translation into Norwegian. He resides in Murfreesboro, Tennessee.

Steven M. Bragg, CPA, CMA, CIA, CDP, CSP, CPM, CPIM, has been the chief financial officer or controller of four companies, as well as a consulting manager at Ernst & Young. He received a master's degree in finance from Bentley College and an MBA from Babson College. He has also written *Just-in-Time Accounting, Advanced Accounting Systems, Financial Analysis, Outsourcing, Accounting Best Practices*, and *Managing Explosive Corporate Growth*, and has coauthored *Controllership* and *The Controller's Function*. Mr. Bragg resides in Englewood, Colorado.

Contents

Preface

This book has been written for business owners and managers who want to refine the sales and operations of their companies. It provides detailed information about how to plan for and integrate all departments, analyze markets, forecast sales, set pricing levels, manage inventories, and outsource selected functions—in short, all of the key sales and operations information required to operate a small business.

Chapter 1 covers the basic planning process, including the formulation of strategy and the linkage of it to a set of tactics that will force all departments to work in concert to achieve that strategy. This is a key area that many small business owners do not address in sufficient detail; we walk the reader through this important process to make it as easy as possible.

Chapter 2 discusses incorporating pricing information into a forecast, segmented by market, that shows what sales volume to expect by product. This is a difficult area for a small business to do properly and can be disastrous if forecasts are far from actual sales experience. We demonstrate several forecasting methods that remove some of the uncertainty from the forecasting process.

Chapter 3 describes marketing analysis. This includes the examination and selection of the most appropriate distribution channels, the examination of competitors within the marketplace, and how one's products can find a competitive position with this market that will ensure a reasonable return on one's investment.

Chapter 4 moves to the issue of pricing. We describe the basic rules of pricing and how to include a product's cost in the formulation of price. We also discuss the issue of how to react to a market that balks at what it feels is an excessively high price. We note how pricing fits into the strategic plan and provide a master checklist of key factors that affect pricing.

Chapter 5 addresses the key operational issue of how to produce to the forecast at the lowest possible cost, while keeping the corporate investment in machinery and inventory to a minimum. We cover the uses of perpetual inventory systems, picking, and backflushing to retain tight control over the inventory, while also noting the advantages and disadvantages of the material requirements planning, manufacturing resources planning, and just-in-time systems in running the flow of materials through the production facility.

Chapter 6 addresses the issue of when to outsource company functions to suppliers, why this is useful, when not to employ this option, and how it can fit into a company's strategic planning. Though outsourcing has become a significant management option, it must be used with care to ensure the best possible results.

Chapter 7 notes how a board of advisors can assist a business owner or manager in running a company, as well as how to pick the correct mix of advisors, organize them, and make them work together. This is a crucial issue, especially for a company that is growing at a rapid rate and needs quality advice regarding what pitfalls to avoid and what steps to take in order to ensure continuing success.

Chapter 8 addresses the problem of business valuation, which is a problem every businessperson wants to have if all of the problems outlined in the preceding chapters have been overcome—how to determine the correct price for one's business. We also turn the issue around and address proper valuations for the acquisition of other companies and the methods one can use to formulate these valuations.

Chapter 9 covers the fascinating topic of rapid growth—why it is difficult to survive a bout of rapid growth and how to maintain control over operations through cash flow analysis, budgeting, and control systems. We also cover the particular issues related to management and ownership that cause friction during explosive growth situations and conclude with a brief overview of the specific problems that growth brings to each major corporate function.

The most effective way to use this book is as a reference source. We suggest that you first read the book through once, implementing the concepts section by section; it is not casual reading but rather a manual, intended for a reading-doing-reading-doing approach. Then, when you have trouble or concerns in a particular area, consult the specific chapter addressing that problem to find solutions.

Though not everything covered in a business school MBA curriculum is covered here, the most relevant topics are; therefore, the book serves as an update for those who have business school training and an introduction to many business concepts for those who have not.

Best wishes for improving, implementing, and benefiting from your decisions—and for making lots of money.

E. James Burton, Ph.D.
Steven M. Bragg
December 2000

Sales and Operations for Your Small Business

Preparing to Operate the Business

Chapter 1

Planning

Everyone plans! Every businessperson looks forward in time and has in mind those things that need to be accomplished for the betterment of the business. These thoughts are specific and personal to the planner; they focus on the areas of major interest to you, rather than cover the whole business (marketing people focus on marketing, finance people on finance, etc.). Such plans are often based on "guesstimates" rather than on factual data. Unless communicated, your thoughts as the planner will not be of much use to other people in the business or serve as motivating tools for others.

Planning, which has as its prescribed end a business plan, should be practical rather than conceptual. When a business plan is written, it is available to all potential users both inside and outside the business. The process of recording thoughts causes the planner to carefully develop schedules to support any estimates or projections being made. The plan becomes a goal-setting device for the rest of the business as well.

The process of writing also spurs one to consider all areas of the organization and integrate them into the plan. The plan is available not only for internal users but also for external users, who may be considering funding the business, or for other external needs such as regulation.

A major part of the material contained in this chapter is abbreviated from E. James Burton *Total Business Planning: A Step-by-Step Guide with Forms* (3rd ed.) (John Wiley & Sons, 1999). You may wish to consult this book for a fuller discussion of various points.

There are at least seven good reasons why you need a business plan.

1. A business plan is an effective management tool for making major decisions. It sets out in detail what you intend to do and how you intend to do it, and serves as the framework for making decisions on how to accomplish the established objectives.
2. A business plan is an effective means for measuring actual performance. By comparing periodic measurements of accomplishment with expectations, you can determine how effectively the business is performing.
3. A business plan is a basis for rewarding performance. If individuals have been assigned responsibilities, and the accomplishment of those responsibilities can be measured, then appropriate and effective rewards can be determined.
4. A business plan helps motivate managers who have contributed to its development. Once a manager has "signed up" to the business plan, it is in that manager's best interest to see to it that the plan is accomplished.
5. A business plan is an educational tool. The process of developing a business plan helps the members of the team better understand the components involved and how they work together.
6. A business plan is a means of communicating expectations and demonstrating results. It informs personnel as to what is expected of them and how they will be measured. It shows them the results of their work according to the plan.
7. A business plan is a good way to verify assumptions regarding the resources needed to run a business. For example, if the plan specifies a massive jump in sales, the plan should specify the personnel, working capital, and facilities needed to accomplish that increase, along with the funds needed to do so.

Process versus Document

Much of the value of a business plan derives from the process one goes through to develop it. A business planning process is a combination of brainstorming, daydreaming, research, analysis, communications, and position-paper writing. If implemented properly, a business planning process provides an opportunity for every level of management to be involved in determining how that business will be conducted over a period of time. A business plan has been described as a written document that spells out in detail where the company's business is and where it is intended to go. It should allow the management team to identify opportunities and threats, recognize strengths and weaknesses, reconcile conflicting views, and arrive at a set of agreed-upon objectives, goals, and tactics in a systematic, realistic manner. As one dissects the components involved in that definition, it becomes obvious that a great deal of effort and time are necessary to construct a good business plan.

A business planning process is like a pyramid. At the top of the pyramid is a senior management team that must decide on key issues to guide the business through a long planning future. Below the senior management team is a larger tier of management. This tier expands upon the concepts put forth by the senior management team, building an increasingly more detailed plan of how these concepts should be accomplished. At each additional management level, the number of people involved increases and the planning becomes more detailed. (See Figure 1.1.)

Even in a smaller business, which may have only a few involved decision makers, the business planning process can be very revealing. As the key decision makers in the business begin to communicate their beliefs as to "what business we are in" and the philosophy under which the business ought to be run, there are often significant disagreements or misunderstandings that need to be resolved. The business planning process usually brings these misunderstandings or disagreements to the surface so that they can be worked on and a consensus can be reached.

Definitions

A common set of definitions will facilitate the understanding of the process in the plan being discussed here. The following list of terms and definitions may be helpful:

FIGURE 1.1

Planning Pyramid

Vision. The view of the future of the organization, which stresses what the visionary wants the organization to become. It is the integration and synthesis of information with dreams.

Philosophy. The set of basic beliefs that establish the parameters (boundaries of behavior) for the business and its personnel. It is a statement of what the business does and does not do. A statement of philosophy often begins with "We believe ..." and follows with "therefore ..."

Mission statement. The mission statement is the primary focus of the business and answers the question, "What business are we in?"

Strategy. A method or course of action for dealing with competitors. It can be proactive or reactive. It answers questions such as "Who else is in this business and how do we relate to them?"

Objective. Objectives are the aim or end of an action, the results to be accomplished. For the business as a whole, the objectives answer the question, "Where do we want to go?"

Status. The status is an assessment of the present position of the business and answers the question, "Where are we?"

Goals. Goals are the ends toward which a particular unit of the business strives; they are a step toward accomplishing an objective. For a particular unit of the business, goals answer the question, "Where do we, as a part of the business, want to go in keeping with the overall objectives of the business?"

Tactics. Tactics are methods of using resources to reach goals. They help to answer the question, "How do we get there?"

Projections. Projections are quantitative assessments and estimates of the results expected from the use of various tactics. These answer the question, "How will we know when we are there?"

Budgets. The quantification of the plan. It should show expected benefits (in financial terms) and the costs needed to achieve those benefits. It should be driven by the plan rather than driving the plan.

Planning Process: Levels One through Nine

Of course, you will need to modify your planning process according to the type and the size of the business involved; still, it is possible to lay out a generalized framework within which the planning process can be developed. The planning process can be thought of as a nine-level process. (See Figures 1.2 and 1.3.)

Level One

The first level in the planning process is the creation of a vision. The word *creation* was chosen with care because the visioning process is perhaps more art than science. Visioning is about seeing and becoming—seeing what others have not, cannot, or will not see and becoming what you want to become without being unduly hampered by what you already are.

FIGURE 1.2

Levels

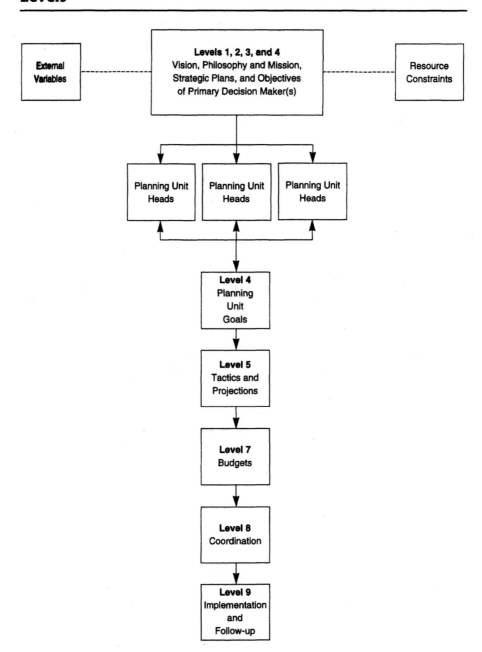

Source: E. James Burton, *Total Business Planning: A Step-by-Step Guide with Forms* (3rd ed.) (New York: John Wiley & Sons, 1999). Reprinted by permission of John Wiley & Sons, Inc.

FIGURE 1.3

Planning Process

Group		Level
Senior Management	Vision	1
Senior Management	Philosophy/Mission	2
Senior Management	Strategic Planning	3
Senior Management	Corporate Objectives	4
Planning Unit Management	Status/Goals	5
Planning Unit Supervisors	Tactics/Projections	6
Budget Heads	Budgets	7
Plan Coordinator	Coordination	8
Everyone	Implementation and Follow-up	9

The time horizon for a vision depends on the industry, the business, and the period in history. However, visions tend to be of closer chronological proximity than not too many years ago. Change happens too fast and there are too many uncontrollable variables for many people to be comfortable looking much past five years into the future. Creating and accomplishing a vision requires both passion and hard work and there are really no good models because each is, by nature, quite distinct.

Visions are often the work of a solitary visionary, but they need not be so. In fact, if a group can create the dream, you are actually ahead of the game because there are fewer people to whom you will have to sell the vision. Usually, the vision comes from the senior management group. It cannot be rushed, and it normally cannot be confined to a specific time frame. It develops at what appears to be its own pace. However, spending focused time considering the vision will improve the possibility of actually articulating one. There are some visioning questions in Appendix A at the end of this chapter.

Level Two

The second level in a planning process is the development of the philosophy and mission of the business. Often, management of the business will have unpublished philosophy and mission statements. For the long-range growth and development of the business, it is important that each of these items be specifically developed and written down so that they can be used by other people within the business for guidance.

The development of the philosophy and the mission statement are the responsibility of the senior management team. The senior management team (even if it consists of only one person—you) should take the time to consider the development of the philosophy and the mission statement in written form. There are forms and questions in the appendices to this chapter that will be helpful in the development of a philosophy statement and a mission statement.

Level Three

The strategic planning portion of the planning process focuses on how to position a company within a market, based on the presence, market position, and strategic advantages of other competitors in that market. Here are some of the issues to consider, which should be noted in summary format in the form shown in Figure 1.5:

- *The market positioning of other companies.* Within each market, there will be a few larger companies, such as Wal-Mart, that are squarely positioned to sell in large volumes and use volume-related efficiencies to drive down costs and prices. Around these companies are positioned others that service specific market niches, such as Rolex for high-end watches. These niche companies are either positioned to provide very high levels of service, or attend to the needs of specific geographic locations that are not serviced by anyone else, or are protected by patents or copyrights, and so can provide a specific product with impunity until their legal protection runs out. A company must survey the strategic landscape to see what competitors occupy each of these portions of the market and decide where it can most profitably find a place. (See Figure 1.4.)
- *Market moves being made by competitors.* The strategic landscape is never quiescent. Instead, companies are constantly acting to shift the competitive situation in their favor, to which other companies

FIGURE 1.4

Product Matrix Analysis

Value Analysis Grid

Planning Unit _____

To be completed by: _____

Product/Service _____

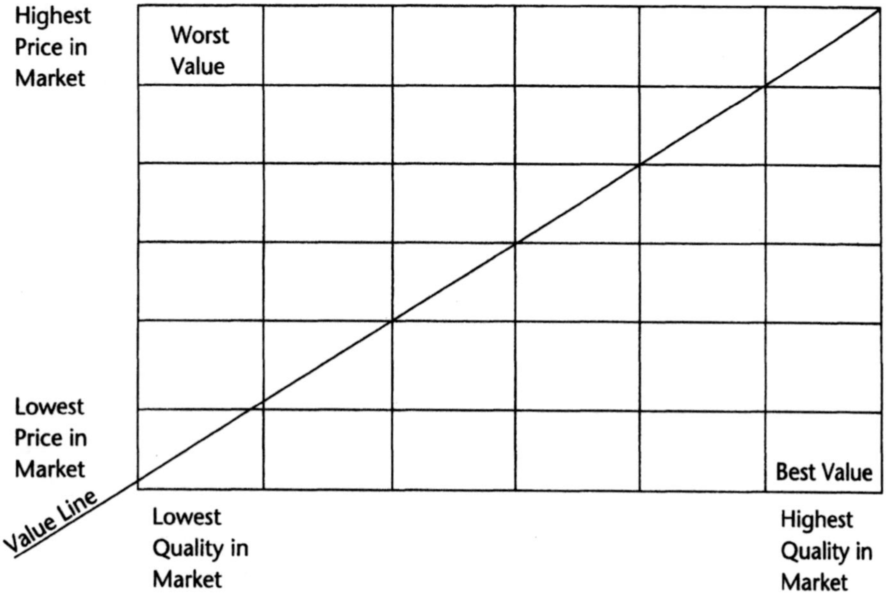

Indicate your idea of where your company's products or services fit in the grid by placing an * in the appropriate box. Indicate where competitors' products or services are on the grid as well.

Source: E. James Burton, *Total Business Planning: A Step-by-Step Guide with Forms* (3rd ed.) (New York: John Wiley & Sons, 1999). Reprinted by permission of John Wiley & Sons, Inc.

must respond, which creates further changes in the situation. If a company has good sources of marketing intelligence, it can take advantage of the moves made by other companies to improve its own positioning. For example, if it knows a competitor has just been purchased and the new owner is unwilling to invest in the business, or if the competitor has just acquired a large amount of

FIGURE 1.5

Strategic Factors Analysis

Customer/Client   Product/Service

	Rank					
Companies	Price	Quality	Delivery			

Summary

_____

_____

_____

_____

_____

Source: E. James Burton, *Total Business Planning: A Step-by-Step Guide with Forms* (3rd ed.) (New York: John Wiley & Sons, 1999). Reprinted by permission of John Wiley & Sons, Inc.

debt to fund an internal management buyout, then the company can probably gain an advantage, by either rolling out new products or starting a price war, because it knows the competitor does not have the wherewithal to respond to these competitive moves. (See Figures 1.5 and 1.6.)

FIGURE **1.6**

Strategic Factors Analysis—Suggestions for Use

1. Identify specific customer/client or a specific customer/client group. Insert in upper left corner.
2. Identify specific product/service to be offered. Insert in upper right corner.
3. Identify the strategic factors considered important to the identified group in suggestion 1. Enter these as column headings along with *Price, Quality,* and *Delivery.*
4. Rank these strategic factors in order of importance, and enter your numerical results into the column headings labeled *Rank.*
5. Compare answers with others and attempt a consensus.
6. List yourself as the first entry under *Companies;* then, in descending order of market share, continue with a list of your competitors.
7. Compare answers with others and attempt a consensus.
8. Insert numbers into the matrix indicating each competitor's ranking with respect to each strategic factor.
9. Compare answers with others and attempt a consensus.
10. Identify rankings which are likely to be subject to attempts at change or which may be likely to change due to economic environment factors. Identify direction of such changes with arrows.
11. Compare answers with others and attempt a consensus.
12. In the space provided, write a short summary of the above described situation.

Source: E. James Burton, *Total Business Planning: A Step-by-Step Guide with Forms* (3rd ed.) (New York: John Wiley & Sons, 1999). Reprinted by permission of John Wiley & Sons, Inc.

- *Changes in customer requirements.* It is possible that customer requirements that drive the positioning of companies within the market will change from time to time, which can upset the relative positions of the companies in the market. For example, when personal computer (PC) users decided that it was acceptable to order computers directly from the manufacturer, Dell Computer was perfectly positioned to take advantage of this shift, vaulting it past Compaq and IBM to become the largest PC manufacturer. Also, a company can deliberately cause these changes in customer requirements by developing alternative products, features, delivery systems, or other improvements from the customer's perspective, and then marketing these changes to customers until they adopt them en masse, which forces competitors to follow suit. (See Figure 1.7.)

FIGURE 1.7

Strategic Plan of Action

With specific reference to your competitors, what do you most want to accomplish?
(State the accomplishments as specific results.)

1. _____

2. _____

3. _____

What course of action will you follow to cause these to happen?

1. a. _____

   b. _____

   c. _____

2. a. _____

   b. _____

   c. _____

3. a. _____

   b. _____

   c. _____

Source: E. James Burton, *Total Business Planning: A Step-by-Step Guide with Forms* (3rd ed.) (New York: John Wiley & Sons, 1999). Reprinted by permission of John Wiley & Sons, Inc.

Level Four

Objectives are the key accomplishments that you have set out for the business as a whole during the planning period. It is probably best that no more than four key objectives are stated. If you are able to find the resources to commit to the accomplishment of four significant objectives, and if those objectives are attained in any given period, the business will have had a very good year. By limiting the number of objectives, you will be able to focus on the most important aspects of your undertaking and avoid dissipating your resources.

There is an alternative approach to setting objectives that emphasizes keeping a company's options as wide open as possible by dabbling in a wide range of opportunities; this approach is the reverse of the normal one, which is a tight focus on a small cluster of objectives. This more wide-ranging approach is most useful in industries in which new technologies and niche markets are appearing at a rapid rate. Examples of such industries are cable television systems, fiber-optic data transmission, and any high-technology sector. In these areas, a company cannot possibly anticipate where the most profitable sectors of the market will be in a few years, so they place small investment "bets" on a number of widely varying opportunities. This approach is designed to keep a company in a position to capitalize on its investments or internal research in a number of different areas, while keeping its overall investment as low as possible. Then, when the direction in which the market is turning becomes more clear, the company can drop its investment in those opportunities that are being bypassed by the market and channel more funds and other resources into those areas that lie more squarely in the market's path. Accordingly, this approach is typified by a large number of objectives being pursued at the same time, with frequent reviews and reshufflings of them, in order to match the company's portfolio of ongoing projects and investments to the most recent market developments. (See Figures 1.8, 1.9, and 1.10.)

Level Five

At the fifth level of the business planning process, additional tiers of management are brought in. With a clear explanation from senior management of the philosophy/mission, strategic plans, and objectives

FIGURE 1.8

Product Planning Record

Planning Unit _____

To be completed by: _____

Product _____ For Year of 20___

			Year		
			Present		
1) Units Sold —Actual					
2) —Projected					
3) Unit Sales Price —Actual					
4) —Projected					
5) Unit Variable Cost —Actual					
6) —Projected					
7) Unit Gross Margin —Actual					
8) —Projected					
9) Total Revenue —Actual					
10) —Projected					
11) Promotion Expense —Actual					
12) —Projected					
13)					
14)					
15)					
16)					

Problems may be indicated by:

- Declining number of units sold
- Declining total revenue
- Declining margins

- Increasing price reductions to maintain sales
- Increasing costs as a percentage of sales

- Increasing promotion expense as a percentage of sales
- Significant variances between actuals and projections

Source: E. James Burton, *Total Business Planning: A Step-by-Step Guide with Forms* (3rd ed.) (New York: John Wiley & Sons, 1999). Reprinted by permission of John Wiley & Sons, Inc.

FIGURE 1.9

Salesperson's Sales Forecast for 20XX

Planning Unit _____

To be completed by: _____

Customer _____   Salesperson

Product(s)	Units Projected				
	Quarter 1	Quarter 2	Quarter 3	Quarter 4	Annual
_____					
_____					
_____					
_____					
_____					
_____					
_____					
_____					
_____					
_____					
_____					
_____					
_____					
_____					
Totals					

- Summarize by division
- Summarize by product

Source: E. James Burton, *Total Business Planning: A Step-by-Step Guide with Forms* (3rd ed.) (New York: John Wiley & Sons, 1999). Reprinted by permission of John Wiley & Sons, Inc.

FIGURE 1.10

Sales Forecast Summary for 20XX

Planning Unit _____

To be completed by: _____

	Units Projected				
Product(s)	Quarter 1	Quarter 2	Quarter 3	Quarter 4	Annual
_____					
_____					
_____					
_____					
_____					
_____					
_____					
_____					
_____					
_____					
_____					
_____					
_____					
_____					
Totals					

Source: E. James Burton, *Total Business Planning: A Step-by-Step Guide with Forms* (3rd ed.) (New York: John Wiley & Sons, 1999). Reprinted by permission of John Wiley & Sons, Inc.

of the business, the other managers will be able to assess their present condition (status) and determine the goals for their particular parts of the business. Their goals should support the corporate objectives. Clear statements of these goals are very important to help additional people in the units determine how to meet the objectives.

Level Six

At this point in the planning process, the largest number of people in the business are brought into the process. The people who have to make things happen within the departments should be involved in establishing the "How do we make them happen?" and "What does it look like when they have happened?" parts of the plan. This should be an opportunity for the personnel in the business to put their creativity to use, to look at a number of different tactics, and to examine what the results of using those various tactics will be.

Level Seven

The seventh level of the process is budgeting—both operational budgeting and financial budgeting. Two people—the person charged with facilitating the business plan and the person charged with producing the master budget—often lead this process.

Although the budgeting process is likely to be somewhat specific in every different organization, there are some portions of the process that are reasonably common. Generally, the process starts with a look at the revenue expectations. The things that are in the first six levels of the plan should influence those expectations significantly. From here, the cost budgets can be prepared—cost of goods sold (or services provided) and the operating expense budget, including personnel. (See Figure 1.11.)

The capital budget should also be based on the plans prepared in the first six levels. Those plans should lead to a determination of equipment needs, construction needs, and all of the other items normally found in the capital budget.

With the revenue and expense budgets and the capital budget in place, one can determine a cash budget as well as a pro forma income statement and balance sheet. This will be the quantification of the

FIGURE 1.11

Key Segment Personnel Projections

Planning Unit

Position Title	Number of Employees		Increase (Decrease)
	Current Yr. 20XX	Planning Yr. 20XX	

plans laid out in the first six levels. The detail necessary to accomplish this is too much for this abbreviated discussion.

Level Eight

Ultimately, it is time to take all of the information you have gathered and to put it into a final document. This is the process of coordination.

In the development of the objectives and goals of the business, all participants should keep in mind the eight characteristics of well-stated objectives and goals.

1. *Consistent.* Objectives and goals should be consistent with all of the planning levels previously described as well as any other stated objectives and goals.
2. *Clear.* Objectives and goals should be stated in such a way that the reader understands the writer's intentions.
3. *Concise.* Objectives and goals should focus on one and only one issue so as to avoid confusion and conflict.
4. *Actionable.* Objectives and goals should be stated in such a way that permits specific actions to be taken toward their accomplishment.
5. *Measurable.* Objectives and goals must be subjected to performance standards and, if possible, those standards should be stated in quantitative terms.
6. *Monitorable.* Objectives and goals should be broken into specific segments so that they can be evaluated periodically for accomplishment.
7. *Positive.* Objectives and goals should be stated in active, not passive, terms.
8. *Motivating.* Objectives and goals should have an element of vision and commitment so that they motivate personnel toward higher accomplishment levels.

Level Nine

Implementation and follow-up are critical. Without diligent and prudent implementation, the best plans are to no avail. Therefore, a major part of the planning effort must be devoted to how to make it happen, how to know if it is happening, what to do if it is not happening, and what rewards are appropriate for those who make it happen. These should not be afterthoughts but rather part of the plan.

Although much of the foundational planning occurs at the top of the organization, the majority of the implementation occurs at the "bottom," on an individual basis. Each person must know exactly what is expected of him or her by what date, and how it will be measured. Figures 1.12 and 1.13 are a part of a system devised by the authors for this purpose.

Figures 1.14 and 1.15 are also a part of that system. These are designed to quantify, to the maximum extent possible, the planning outcome expectations. Having a quantitative measurement system allows everyone to grasp quickly how well they are doing against plan and to note where adjustments are needed.

Results can be noted at the individual level, the unit level, and the organization level. Figure 1.16 shows a sample outcome from the quantitative measurement at the organization level.

Putting the measurement in graphic form, much like the standard United Way barometer that is so often used to note progress toward a contribution goal, is very effective. Figure 1.17 illustrates how this is done using the numbers from Figure 1.16.

Following Figure 1.17 is the outline of a business plan. For your specific purpose, you may reorganize, add to, or delete sections of this outline. However, this will serve as a guide for the plan you want to put together.

FIGURE 1.12

Individual Performance Expectations—Summary of Tactics/Action Steps Assigned

Name: _____   Page __ of __
Department: _____·_____   Acknowledged by: _____
                                             Date: _____

Goal ID #	Tactic/Action Step Assigned	Completion Date	Evidence of Completion

Source: E. James Burton, *Total Business Planning: A Step-by-Step Guide with Forms* (3rd ed.) (New York: John Wiley & Sons, 1999). Reprinted by permission of John Wiley & Sons, Inc.

FIGURE 1.13

Individual Performance Expectations—Instructions

_____   _____
Due Date   Planning Facilitator

Each Responsible Manager should complete an Individual Performance Expectations (IPE) sheet for each employee to whom one or more Action Steps has been assigned for one or more Goals.

Primarily, the IPE sheet is a consolidation of information from the Goal Action Plan Sheets. It is intended to help the employee and manager understand and track the Tactics/Action Steps for which an individual is responsible.

As the Responsible Manager, you should:

1. Complete the Name and Department information.
2. List the Goal ID #, the Tactic/Action Step Assigned, the Completion Date by which this step should be done, and the Evidence of Completion for *each* item assigned to this person. This information can be taken from the Goal Action Plan Sheets.
3. Complete the "Page __ of __" indicators for each page for each person.
4. Give a copy of each Employee's IPE to that Employee and discuss the expectations.
5. Have each employee sign and date (Acknowledged by and Date) the original IPE and return it to you. The employee should retain a copy.
6. Keep a copy and give the original to the Planning Coordinator by the Due Date.
7. At least quarterly, review the IPE sheets with each of your employees as a part of the plan progress review.

Source: E. James Burton, *Total Business Planning: A Step-by-Step Guide with Forms* (3rd ed.) (New York: John Wiley & Sons, 1999). Reprinted by permission of John Wiley & Sons, Inc.

FIGURE 1.14

Goal Weighting and Progress Chart

FYE: _____

Due Date   Planning Facilitator

Please complete the indicated columns and return to the Planning Facilitator on or before the Due Date.

Responsible Person: _____

Columns to be Completed
| 1 | 2 | 3 | 4 | 5 | 6 | 7 | 8 | 9 | 10 | 11 | 12 |

Corp. Obj. No.	Weight to Objective	Goal No.	Weight to Goal	Cumulative Completion Percentage*							
				Exp. 1st Qtr.	Act. 1st Qtr.	Exp. 2nd Qtr.	Act. 2nd Qtr.	Exp. 3rd Qtr.	Act. 3rd Qtr.	Exp. 4th Qtr.	Act. 4th Qtr.
										100%	
										100%	
										100%	
										100%	
										100%	
										100%	
										100%	
										100%	
										100%	
										100%	
										100%	
										100%	
										100%	
										100%	
XX	XX	XX	100%	XX	XX	XX	XX	XX	XX	XX	XX
Col 1	Col 2	Col 3	Col 4	Col 5	Col 6	Col 7	Col 8	Col 9	Col 10	Col 11	Col 12

*Exp = Expected at beginning of plan year *Act = Actual at end of quarter
Expected columns to be completed fully. Actual columns to be completed at the end of the quarter.

Source: E. James Burton, *Total Business Planning: A Step-by-Step Guide with Forms* (3rd ed.) (New York: John Wiley & Sons, 1999). Reprinted by permission of John Wiley & Sons, Inc.

FIGURE 1.15

Goal Weighting and Progress Chart

FYE: _____

INSTRUCTIONS

Due Date	Planning Facilitator

You have received a summary of all the Goals for your responsibility area with a Goal Identification number assigned and a Goal Weighting and Progress Chart listing all your Goals by Identification Number. If this is not so, please contact the Planning Facilitator immediately.

The Goal Listing Sheet is a summary of the Goals you have established for yourself and your responsibility area. It is for your information.

Goal Weighting and Progress Chart Instructions:

1. Columns 1, 2, and 3 have been completed for you.
2. Looking at your Goal Listing Sheet and considering the weight assigned to the related Corporate Objectives, (Col. 2), assign a weight (portion of 100%) to each listed Goal. Place the assigned weight in Col. 4 beside each Goal number (Col. 3).
3. Note that the sum of all Goal Weights for your Department must be 100%.
4. For each listed Goal, complete Cols. 5, 7, and 9 with the **cumulative** percentage of that Goal which you plan to attain by the end of the indicated quarter. Note that Col. 11 already indicates the planned cumulative percentage completion at the end of the 4th quarter to be 100%.
5. The same sheet will be used at the end of each quarter for you to record the Actual Completion of each Goal. However, at this time, Cols. 6, 8, 10, and 12 should be left blank.
6. When you have completed the above, make a copy of this sheet for your records and return the original to the Planning Facilitator by the Due Date above.

Source: E. James Burton, *Total Business Planning: A Step-by-Step Guide with Forms* (3rd ed.) (New York: John Wiley & Sons, 1999). Reprinted by permission of John Wiley & Sons, Inc.

FIGURE 1.16

Sample Outcome

Objective	Weight	Relative Completion	Year-end Weighted Completion	Variance
Objective 1	20.00%	82.67%	16.53%	−3.47%
Objective 2	30.00%	100.00%	30.00%	0.00%
Objective 3	40.00%	60.00%	24.00%	−16.00%
Objective 4	10.00%	100.00%	10.00%	0.00%
Total	100.00%		80.53%	−19.47%

FIGURE **1.17**

Comparison of Expected to Actual—Sample

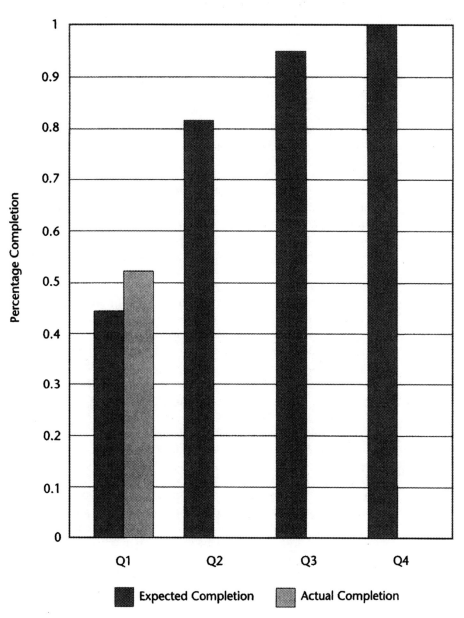

Expected Completion   Actual Completion

Source: E. James Burton, *Total Business Planning: A Step-by-Step Guide with Forms* (3rd ed.) (New York: John Wiley & Sons, 1999). Reprinted by permission of John Wiley & Sons, Inc.

BUSINESS PLAN OUTLINE

1. *Cover sheet* (with appropriate descriptions):
   Business name
   Business address
   Business phone
   Principals
   Date

2. *Sign-up page.* Every manager who helps make the plan should sign it, thereby encouraging commitment to the plan.

3. *Executive summary.* This is what sells someone on reading the remainder of the plan. It should be about two double-spaced, typed pages and contain the essence of the plan. *Remember:* Consider for whom it is written, what is being requested from them, and why they should be interested in doing it.

4. *Table of contents.* Make it specific and complete. Some readers may judge the completeness of the plan from the detail provided in the table of contents.

5. *Major assumptions.* Any assumptions vital to the plan should be stated here. Also include brief contingencies for actions to be taken if the assumptions are violated.

6. *Background section.* If this is a start-up venture, a brief explanation should be made of how the idea (project, product, new territory company, etc.) originated. If this is an operating plan, this section may supplement the major highlights with additional detail in an appendix.

7. *Definition of the business.* It is important that you be able to state succinctly what the business is. This is distinct from what the business does (a listing of functions, products, or services), and should be geared to answer the question: *What need are we meeting?* The philosophy and mission are placed here.

8. *Definition of the market.* Having stated *what* need you are fulfilling, you can now define *who* has that need. Your definition will indicate the target of your marketing effort and will give demographic characteristics. Your market penetration projections should be included along with an analysis of the competition. Your strategic planning assessments will be placed here.

9. *Description of products or services.* Identify needed products or services. The description(s) of the product or services should fully explain to the reader why, given the previously stated information, your products or services will be demanded. You may append catalog sheets, pictures, and so forth. Basically, this is psychographic information—why people will buy your products or services.

10. *Management structure.* Having described the business, the market, and the product, it is time to indicate who will make things happen. A start-up or financing plan will require more detail than will an operating plan. Resumes and other details of personal backgrounds should be left to an appendix. This section should sell two things: *that you have the right people* and *that they are properly organized.*

11. *Objectives, goals, and tactics.* State what you intend to accomplish and how. Include varying amounts of detail based on the purpose of the plan, but focus this section on the "crunch factors." Much of the detail can be placed in the

appendices. Areas of objectives or goals to be covered in this section include (but are not limited to):

a. Sales forecasts.
b. Marketing plans.
c. Manufacturing or servicing plans.
d. Quality assurance plans.
e. Financial plans.

12. *Financial data.* The plan is future oriented. Therefore, this section should focus on projections and pro formas. Historical financial information necessary to understanding the plan should be referenced in an appendix. The items to be included are:

a. Cost–volume–profit analysis.
b. Income projections—pro forma:
   • Monthly for planning year
   • Quarterly for second year
   • Annual for third year
c. Cash flow analysis—pro forma:
   • Monthly for planning year
   • Quarterly for second year
   • Annual for third year

Appendices

Appendices give supporting detail to the content section as well as adding material of interest not otherwise included. If there is proprietary information (patent, research and development, formulas, market research, etc.) the distribution of which you may wish to control, it would be wise to place that information in detachable appendices to include:

1. Narrative history of the company.
2. Management structure (additional resumes, organization charts, etc.).
3. Detail of objectives, goals, and strategies:
   • Products and services
   • Research and development
   • Marketing
   • Manufacturing
   • Administration
   • Finance

4. Historical financial information (three to five years if possible).
5. Tax returns (three to five years if possible).
6. Letters of recommendation or endorsement.
7. Report forms and schedules.

Plan Verification Steps

Having completed the plan, one should first review it for inconsistencies prior to finalizing it. In this section, several areas in which plans commonly have shortcomings are noted. They are as follows:

- *Sales.* The most common reason why so many business plans closely resemble science fiction is that management has not carefully reviewed the basis for its sales predictions. Because sales volume forms the basis for many other company activities, such as purchasing levels, staffing, and investments in facilities, the verification of prospective sales information must be as detailed as possible. This should include not only the volumes of expected sales in units, but also the incremental price points at which those sales are expected to occur. When reviewing this information, verify the extent to which the company expects to change its market share; a large increase in sales probably necessitates an increase in market share (unless the market itself is increasing), and grabbing more market share can be quite a difficult endeavor to accomplish. If the forecasted sales level on which the plan is based is substantially higher than sales from the prior year, then it is best to factor into the plan a secondary level of greatly reduced activity, in case some or all of the extra sales do not actually materialize. This usually involves shifting most planned activities that require funding to as far in the future as possible, while implementing noncash activities as soon as possible.
- *Capacity.* The scope of expansion outlined in a business plan may not be achievable, given the current capacity of company facilities and equipment. Unfortunately, this major item is sometimes not considered when the plan is being assembled. At its worst, this can result in new sales for which a company has no way of meeting its production requirements, which has the additional result of rapidly increasing shipment backlogs, dissatisfied customers

(because they are not receiving shipments on time), and rush charges to obtain the machinery and facilities that should have already been outlined in the plan. Accordingly, the capacity levels specified in the plan should be reasonable, assuming an adequate amount of machinery downtime for maintenance, and use run rates that are based on historically accurate information. This analysis may result in additional funding requirements to obtain more facilities and machinery.

- *Funding.* Many activities in a plan require funding. These can be capital expenditures, payroll costs for new employees, or additions to working capital. Whatever the reason, the plan will be inoperative if there are not enough available funds to complete the plan's goals. Accordingly, the plan should include specific targets for obtaining either equity funding, debt financing, or increased cash flows from internal operations. These cash inflows should coincide with or precede any activities that require funds, so the timing of these activities is critical.

- *Working capital.* A major increase in sales volume will have a major impact on a company's investment in accounts receivable and inventory, since these two assets will increase to service extra sales. For example, if invoice payment terms are 30 days, then any increase in sales volume must be funded by the company for 30 days before customers pay for the invoices. When sales increase markedly, a company that does not properly plan for the coincident increase in working capital will find itself suddenly short of cash. To avoid this, the plan should include either the acquisition of debt or equity or a change in the method of operations that results in either shorter invoice payment terms or a better inventory management system, such as material requirements planning (MRP) or just-in-time (JIT), which require a smaller investment in inventory.

- *Inconsistent goals.* Individual employees will generally notice if their portions of the business plan contain inconsistent goals, and will tell the management group, which can make the necessary alterations to the plan. However, this is not so obvious when inconsistent goals are spread among different people or departments. For example, the accounting staff may be asked to reduce the amount of bad debt, which it does by cutting back on the credit levels granted to customers. However, this goal goes directly against the wishes of the sales staff, if that department has been given the goal of increasing the average amount of sales to existing customers. Such offsetting goals can cause strife between departments and certainly do not contribute to the accomplishment of corporate goals while managers bicker. Fixing this issue requires a careful comparison of all goals that have been laid out within the plan and should involve the review of all department managers, because they are in the best position to see if some other part of the company will be working on conflicting activities.

- *Prioritization of goals.* In any plan, there are a few extremely important goals and a number of others that are not so critical to the accomplishment of a company's key objectives. If the senior management group does not prioritize these goals for the people who must complete them, then the lower-level people in the company are forced to guess which ones to complete first, and their order of priority will probably not match the one that the senior management team would assign. Also, the staff may assume that all goals are due for completion immediately if they are not prioritized, which will cause them to put off other key tasks until the goals are done. Finally, some goals may be contingent on the earlier completion of other goals, so some employees may find that goals they have already accomplished must now be redone, based on the later completion of other goals whose results were supposed to feed into their work. The senior management group can eliminate all of these issues by setting clear priorities regarding the order of completion of specific tasks.

- *Capacity to complete goals.* If the staff is inundated with goals to accomplish, they may become so overwhelmed that no goals will be completed, they will be drastically delayed, or the staff's current work will suffer while they strive to complete the extra work. To keep these things from happening, one should carefully review the time needed by the people to whom goals have been assigned to see if they can realistically accomplish the work they have been assigned. If not, then either the number of goals must be scaled back or extra personnel should be hired to take on the extra work.

Summary

Planning is a function carried out in varying degrees by people as individuals as well as people banded together to form organizations or businesses. Most plans are conceptualizations of what a person intends to do in the short- or long-term future. A business plan operates in the same manner. Unless written, however, the plan may be of little use externally or even internally. The physical process of writing a plan encourages consideration of most of the elements of a good plan.

Creating a business plan is an ongoing, continuous process, the implementation of which will determine how the business will be run over time. The plan should be originated from the top down, with upper management providing direction and objectives and lower levels of management fleshing out detail and definition.

The step-by-step generation is done in nine levels. Level one is the creation of a vision of what the business can and should become. Level two is the development of philosophy/mission. Level three is the strategic assessment of the competitive environment. Level four is the statement of the major objectives for the firm or business. Level five is the setting of the goals for the particular parts of the business. Level six is the assimilation of the people who have to execute the plan to establish how it will be made to happen. Level seven is the generation of the budgets to show the financial picture coincident to the plan. Level eight is the generation of a tangible document, formalizing the plan as envisioned. The objectives of the business should be consistent, clear, concise, actionable, measurable, monitorable, positive, and motivating. Level nine is implementation and follow-up on what has been planned.

While there is no set format for a business plan, many text writers offer a variety of suggestions. What they all seem to have in common is a structured format for the presentation of how the business got here, what assumptions were being made, where it intends to go, and how it expects to get there.

Remembering that the business plan may also serve the purpose of trying to "sell" the business to bankers, investors, and potential trade creditors, it is best to write for the specific audience expected to read the document. You may wish to tailor a version of the plan to the specific audience. This can be done by changing the emphasis and detail in certain parts of the plan. If, for example, the business is seeking a short-term loan from a bank, the firm's liquidity and cash flow prospects should be emphasized (especially if they are favorable).

Appendix A: Visioning Questions

1. What are our current core competencies _____
   _____

2. What can we leverage to build our future?_____
   _____

3. How will the political environment in which we operate change in the next 10 years, and what impact will this have on our organization? _____
   _____

4. How will the business environment in which we operate change in the next 10 years, and what impact will this have on our organization? _____
   _____

5. What technological changes will impact our organization? What will these changes do to us?_____
   _____

6. How can we capitalize on them? _____
   _____

7. Who are the people that will lead the organization over the next 10 years? _____
   _____

8. What are their best skills?_____
   _____

9. Where will they want to take the organization? _____
   _____

10. How big should the organization be? _____
    _____

11. What resources will be necessary to achieve this size? _____
    _____

12. What knowledge and skills do we organizationally possess that produce a competitive advantage for us? _____
    _____

Source: E. James Burton, *Total Business Planning: A Step-by-Step Guide with Forms* (3rd ed.) (New York: John Wiley & Sons, 1999). Reprinted by permission of John Wiley & Sons, Inc.

Appendix B: History Questionnaire

To be completed by:_____

Completing these questions will help to show how we became what we are and why we are positioned to do what we have planned to do. _____

1. Date of company's founding. _____

   _____

   _____

2. Original founder(s) of business, name of business, location of business, and purpose of business. _____

   _____

   _____

3. Changes in name, location, and/or purpose, along with corresponding dates.

   _____

   _____

   _____

4. Major economic or environmental events which have affected company.

   _____

   _____

   _____

5. Dates and explanations of major additions to or divestitures of business.

   _____

   _____

   _____

6. Major obstacles and problems the business has faced. _____

   _____

   _____

   _____

7. Turning points causes of greatest periods of growth and profitability.

   _____

   _____

   _____

Source: E. James Burton, *Total Business Planning: A Step-by-Step Guide with Forms* (3rd ed.) (New York: John Wiley & Sons, 1999). Reprinted by permission of John Wiley & Sons, Inc.

Appendix C: Status Quo Questionnaire

To be completed by:_____

1. If the company operates in the coming year in the same manner as this year, identify those areas under your budgeting control (budget lines) which:

   a. Must be increased

   _____

   b. Could stay the same

   _____

   c. Are targets for cost reductions

   _____

2. Again assuming the present methods of operations:

   a. Identify two conditions over which you have little control that keep your area from making a greater profit contribution.

   _____

   _____

   b. State two changes which you have (or can get) authority to initiate that should make your area more profitable.

   _____

   _____

   c. By what date(s) could the above changes reasonably be made?

   _____

Source: E. James Burton, *Total Business Planning: A Step-by-Step Guide with Forms* (3rd ed.) (New York: John Wiley & Sons, 1999). Reprinted by permission of John Wiley & Sons, Inc.

Appendix D: Thirty Questions to Assist With Strategic Planning

1. Who are our five major customers (or classes of customers)?

    a. _____

    b. _____

    c. _____

    d. _____

    e. _____

2. What are the common characteristics of these five?

    a. _____

    b. _____

    c. _____

3. Why do they buy our product?

    a. _____

    b. _____

    c. _____

4. Who are three potential customers (or classes of customers) who do not currently do business with us?

    a. _____

    b. _____

    c. _____

5. Why don't these three do business with us?

    a. _____

    b. _____

    c. _____

6. Are there any obvious ethnic, age, religious, gender, or other biases in our customer base?

    a. _____

    b. _____

7. What is our most effective sales channel?

   a. _____

   b. _____

   c. _____

8. What products are our three greatest revenue producers?

   a. _____

   b. _____

   c. _____

9. What products are our three greatest profit producers?

   a. _____

   b. _____

   c. _____

10. If customers could not buy what we sell (even from a competitor) what would they do?

    a. _____

    b. _____

    c. _____

    d. _____

    e. _____

Demographics—Who buys?

11. Are our products purchased primarily by any particular age group?

    _____

12. Are our products purchased primarily by any specific ethnic group?

    _____

13. Are our products purchased primarily by one gender?

    _____

14. Are our products purchased primarily within any geographic area(s)?

    _____

15. Are our products purchased primarily by any income level group?

    _____

16. Are sales of our product(s) tied to sales or use of any other products?

_____

17. Are sales of our product tied largely to any occupational category?

_____

18. What is the education level of our primary purchasers?

_____

19. Who (according to the above categories) are the heaviest users of our products?

_____

Psychographics—Why do they buy?

20. What are the benefits each class of customer (see above) derives from using product?

_____

_____

21. Which *advertising* has been most effective?

_____

_____

22. Whose *endorsement* might cause a person to buy our product(s)?

_____

_____

23. What types of *packaging* have produced the most sales?

_____

_____

24. What is the buyer's *hot button?*

_____

_____

Channels—Where do they buy?

25. Which distribution channel produces the most sales revenue?

_____

_____

26. Which distribution channel produces the most gross profit?

_____

_____

27. What has been the greatest change competitors have made in distribution channels?

_____

_____

28. What has been the most effective change we have made in distribution channels?

_____

_____

29. Why was the change (in question 28) so effective?

_____

_____

30. Is there a level in the distribution link which can be eliminated?

_____

_____

Source: E. James Burton, *Total Business Planning: A Step-by-Step Guide with Forms* (3rd ed.) (New York: John Wiley & Sons, 1999). Reprinted by permission of John Wiley & Sons, Inc.

Appendix E: Internal Data Monitoring

Item Monitored	Last Period	Current Period	Desired Pro Forma
Financial			
1. Profit Margin (Earnings/Sales)			
2. Asset Turnover (Sales/Assets)			
3. Capital Structure (Assets/Equity)			
4. Return on Equity [(1) × (2) × (3)]			
5. Accounts Receivable Turnover (Sales/Accounts Receivable)			
6. Accounts Payable Turnover (Purchases/Accounts Payable)			
7. Current Ratio (Current Assets/Current Liabilities)			
Operational*			
8.			
9.			

* Examples of operational data to be monitored might include:
- Backlog
- Rejects
- Downtime
- Calls received

Source: E. James Burton, *Total Business Planning: A Step-by-Step Guide with Forms* (3rd ed.) (New York: John Wiley & Sons, 1999). Reprinted by permission of John Wiley & Sons, Inc.

Chapter 2

Forecasting

As stated in the previous chapter, any businessperson who seriously intends to improve the likelihood of success engages in some form of planning. Because one does not know with certainty what the future will bring, the ongoing process of making decisions will involve estimates and projections based on past experiences, others' advice, and some old "seat-of-the-pants" guessing. Like personal plans for the weekend, plans for the future are based on forecasts. The forecast provides the skeleton that you flesh out with operating, financial, and sales expectations.

Forecasting, with all its potential mathematical complexities, statistical manipulations, and scientific underpinnings, still has a little magic and intuition to it. The weather forecast for the weekend may be conducted on a grand, "scientific," scale with weather satellites, color weather radar, and sophisticated modeling, but whether it will rain at the cottage on Saturday is still just an educated guess. Likewise, a forecast of the economy and the market will be both scientific and intuitive.

In business, forecasting is often associated with quantitative projections of specific numbers such as sales, gross profits, operating expenses, and so on. Certainly these projections are a necessary element. However, there is a qualitative component as well, which does not lend itself to numeric outcomes but is equally essential.

Forecasting is a learned skill; it is the assimilation of data into a usable estimation of what the future will *probably* be. Better data does not guarantee better forecasts but it does improve the probability.

Good forecasts are the result of two elements: good data and meaningful analysis. These two elements are the foundation of the four basic steps of good forecasting:

- Compilation of accurate fundamental data (sometimes called the benchmark)
- Preparation of the data for analysis purposes
- Application of one or more forecasting methods to analyze the data
- Application of sound judgment and intuition to develop the forecast

Because there are many good books written on the mathematical/statistical aspects of forecasting, which is a complex and time-consuming subject on its own, we will discuss these matters briefly and refer you to other sources to deal with those complexities. This chapter focuses on *using* forecasts.

Some representative references you may want to consult for help with the "math" part of forecasting are (from simple to complicated):

- *Budgeting Fundamentals for Nonfinancial Executives and Managers,* Allen Sweeny and John Wisener, Jr., McGraw-Hill Paperbacks.
- *Budgeting for Profit,* John C. Camillus, Chilton Better Business Services.
- *Business Cycles and Forecasting,* Carl A. Danten and Lloyd M. Valentine, Southwestern Publishing Company.
- The instruction manual from your computer spreadsheet package.
- *Information for Decision Making: Quantitative and Behavioral Decisions* (2nd ed.), Alfred Rappaport, editor, Prentice-Hall.

Initially, you have to decide what you are trying to forecast:

- A short-term projection—less than a year
- An intermediate plan—two to five years
- A long-term commitment of over five years

At first, it seems unlikely that you will try to forecast the future for more than five years. But some large, capital-intensive businesses must forecast beyond that period. An electric utility, for example, which may invest billions of dollars in just one power plant, faces construction cycles of five to seven years. At the time of completion, the company hopes to have adequate demand to pay both a return *of* its investments and a return *on* its investment.

Closer to home, you may have to look five to seven years out if you are starting from scratch to research and develop a significant new product.

Once the planning or forecasting horizon is established, you have to make the second essential decision: "What is it we want to forecast?" For the power plant, as with many products, the question may have many answers:

- The peak and average demand for power by year, until project retirement
- The regulatory environment established by the government and how much it will allow to be recovered through rates during construction
- The projected costs from completion of construction through the operating life of the plant
- The environmental concerns faced in the generation of electricity from other energy sources

These questions may not seem to be comparable to your forecasting problems. However, upon closer examination, the concerns are not dissimilar. For the smaller business, the forecasting demands might be:

- Peak and average demand for the product.
- What government regulation might be imposed (quotas, import restriction, tariffs, etc.)?
- What will the investment market be like—what will money cost?
- What design changes or product innovations may result?
- What air or water pollution problems may the business processes encounter (e.g., waste disposals)?
- What can we expect from competitors?

This series of concerns points up the need to forecast the external environment. The external environment consists of all those factors outside the business that may affect the ability of the business to produce, market, and sell a product or service.

While the external environment has an impact on the business, it is not the only environment that the business must survey. The business is also affected by many internal forces:

1. *Labor costs.* Some of the considerations to be included in the forecasts are:
   - Employee/benefits-related costs.
   - Government requirements.
   - Safety costs.
   - Hours of work required.
   - Automation impacts.
   - Unions impacts.
   - Productivity changes.
   - Turnover/retirement.
2. *Material Costs.* In this case, other elements must be evaluated to make an estimate of future costs:
   - Availability—whether resources are scarce or plentiful.
   - Transportation.
   - Substitute commodities.
   - Disposal of wastes.
   - Product redesign/engineering changes.
   - Cost reductions.
   - Scrap and rework.
3. *Overhead Costs.* Some of the concerns involved include:
   - Taxes.
   - Utilities.
   - Maintenance/building repair.
   - Cleaning.
   - Materials handling.
   - Warehousing and shipping.

Compiling Accurate Data

With good information, some insight, and intuition, most people can generate a meaningful forecast. You may have the necessary insight or intuition but still wonder where the information needed for forecasting comes from. It is obtained from the same two environments that affect the future operations of the business: inside sources and outside sources.

Information from Internal Sources

- *Company records.* These records are the basic internal data sources for the firm. Internal company records can be readily and consistently generated by automated or manual manipulations of production, financial, personnel, advertising, inventory, purchasing, and other data.
- *Product sales records.* These can be sorted and arranged by customer, product, sales region, county, city, product class, salesman, individual brand, and other.
- *Sales personnel.* Salesmen and regional sales managers can develop important information at a grassroots level from customers, jobbers, distributors, and other local people such as bankers.

Information from External Sources

- *Government publications of statistical data.* Often, government publications are the original source data used and summarized by other sources. Caution should be used to ensure that the data are the most current available. The government is continuously updating and refining its reports.
- *Secondary sources.* Many business publications, such as *Fortune, The Wall Street Journal, Business Week, Newsweek,* and *U.S. News and World Report,* are first-rate sources of statistical data; however, the information printed in these sources is often derived (and interpreted) from primary government publications. Going to the primary source is preferable.
- *Information and data from trade associations.* This data is compiled and generated from members of the trade association, paid for by members, and generally distributed to members.
- *Trade publications.* Information, data, and analysis are published in trade journals, trade papers, or magazines and consumer publications. It may be provided at no charge or for a subscription fee.
- *Syndicated services.* Again, data, information, and analysis are accumulated by syndicated services, which sell this material to subscribers. Usually, this information is restricted to subscribers.

The phrase "to subscribers only," used by a number of the best publications, makes it sound as if there are few free data sources. However, in a great number of cases, the public library is either a subscriber or may be associated with another library that is a subscriber. Because most libraries are funded through public money, they offer easy and free access to the publications that are limited to "subscribers only." In fact, librarians will always assist in locating relevant, timely data and information. Public libraries, particularly college and university libraries, are great sources of current information.

Preparing the Data for Analysis

A forecast is the end result of a continuous process aimed at predicting the future. Because one cannot consistently predict the future with any certainty, the process has a feedback step built into the procedure to permit you to reconsider the projections based on changed data. Forecasting should be continuous and ongoing and not static. Because the value of any forecast is based on the degree to which it can provide useful information for the decision-making process, the best information about the market and the demands it places on you should be input into the process.

There is no one hard-and-fast forecasting process, but the following eight steps are generally applicable to most forecasting efforts. These can be expanded or contracted to fit your needs.

1. List the basic facts about past trends and forecasts.
2. Establish the causes of changes in past actual demand.
3. Analyze the causes of deviations between previous forecasts and past actuals.
4. Determine factors that are likely to affect future demand.
5. Based only on information available to you *before* that period, generate a forecast for a *past* period. Then measure your accuracy and reliability against the known results. Make any necessary changes to your process until it is an acceptable predictor of the *actual* results of the past period. This allows you, via a trial run approach, to construct a proven effective process on known data.

6. Create a forecast for the future using your revised methodology from step 5.
7. Monitor the performance of the forecast against actual outcomes and determine the causes of variation from the forecast.
8. Revise the forecast when new data or obvious methodology errors appear.

Stating an eight-step process for the generation and use of a forecast makes it appear as if there is a beginning and an end. In reality, it is a continuous process throughout the life of any product and continues through a transition period into new products.

The forecasting process is an especially continuous one for the sales of any new products. When the sales department forecasts sales for a product that has just been released to the market, or will shortly be released, then its best forecasting guess will be based on the sales of similar products. However, this basis may not be sufficient for arriving at an accurate forecast, for a variety of reasons—there are few comparable products on the market or the products already in the market are monopolizing sales, leaving no room for a new contender, or the product's features are so new that there is no realistic basis of comparison. For all of these reasons, the forecasts on such products must be considered unreliable until proven, and so must be compared to actual results every month to see where sales are really tracking. If actual sales vary significantly from estimates, then the sales department should continually revise its forecasts until sales settle down into a recognizable pattern that can then be predicted for many periods into the future.

A continual reexamination of sales forecasts may also be necessary for products that have been in the market for some time but are experiencing sudden shifts in sales, either positive or negative, that are well outside their normal sales boundaries. These changes may be caused by new customers buying the product, fad purchases, or declines in sales due to new competition from other products. In these cases, the products should be placed on a "watch list" that involves a close examination of sales levels, and changes in the forecast as a result of those reviews.

Some of the major external factors to be considered in the forecasting process are:

Competitor/Market Analysis

- The primary data requirement is the size of the market or potential market—locally, regionally, or nationally.
- The number of direct competitors and those producing similar products that may target different parts of the market because of product differentiation.
- The relative position in the market and an analysis of the objectives stated in your business plan.
- Results of any test marketing programs and the information generated concerning national or regional market acceptance.
- Estimation of competitive reaction to product introduction.

In undertaking a test market analysis, you try to estimate what will happen in your target by experimenting in reasonably representative smaller markets. You experiment with different advertising and promotional campaigns and observe the effectiveness of the programs. Getting some actual reactions to plans for the product's introduction market-wide should lessen the risk of product failure. Usually by this stage in the process of product introduction the product is well defined and capable of being produced in quantity.

Often, however, you are interested in opening a retail outlet or providing a service and do not have the luxury (and the considerable expense) associated with test marketing. In such cases, in order to improve the chances of success, you may still wish to conduct a small market survey.

For example, a businessman in a city of 96,000 is considering opening a Scandinavian furniture and accessories store. At present, there is no store of its kind in the city. He has visited most of the specialty stores in the community and has reasonably assured himself that except for a few isolated products in a few stores, he could expect no immediate competition. Although this is interesting, it does not ensure success—it means there is no *current* competition, but it could also mean that someone has tried and failed to provide the product.

What do you do next? Information normally available in the public library may be very helpful to you. A survey of the U.S. Census will give the cities in the United States with populations comparable to that of the city in which you seek to start the business. Next, a review of the telephone directory yellow pages for those cities (also often available in the library) quickly identifies cities with Scandinavian furniture stores. In this manner, a data base of comparable businesses in similar cities can be compiled, with names, addresses, and phone numbers.

The owners of some of these businesses may be willing to share their experiences, if they feel secure that they are not providing a potential competitor with information. If the businesses or cities are not at too great a distance, you can visit them to obtain valuable pricing and marketing information.

In summary, the concerns of the retail store are not unlike the manufacturer:

- Determine if you have competitors and who they are.
- Segment the furniture and accessories market, and settle on the business of Scandinavian furniture and accessories.
- Evaluate the possibility or probability of new entrants into the market segment.

One final consideration is determining how and in what areas the business can compete. If you are entering a market with established competition, you should prepare an evaluation of how and on what variables the competitors compete. This is called Strategic Competitor Assessment and is part of the Strategic Factors Analysis (see Chapter 1, Figures 1.5 and 1.6).

A pertinent question for a Strategic Competitor Assessment is: Do the firms compete on the basis of:

- Costs (cost-plus construction)?
- Price (roofing shingles)?
- Technology (personal computers, watches, and calculators)?
- Service (accounting firms, lawyers, and consultants)?
- Distribution (fast food)?

By discovering the variable of most importance, you will have valuable information on which to base your business plan. In addition, you will know the area of data collection of primary importance to your forecasting needs.

In some areas, technological breakthroughs have occurred with such speed that new products are developed and marketed in a matter of months. The digital wristwatch is such a product. With the rate of innovation and concentration on product features (at low prices) it is difficult to predict future market conditions. The wristwatch market at one time was distinguished by two features: cost and accuracy. With the introduction of sophisticated electronic technologies, the issue of accuracy of movements has been significantly reduced as a differentiable issue. With the tremendous reduction in the costs of technology and the high market competition, prices have been driven down to the level that the product is often considered disposable. It may be cheaper to buy a new watch than to purchase replacement batteries.

Though historical information may show a frequency of product innovation and introduction, this may not be useful in periods of great change. The difficulty may be compounded if the product is subject to seasonal demand. Technological innovations reduced to new product introduction are timed to coincide with high product demand periods.

Another technological innovation consideration is the entry of existing technology into new products and markets. The microprocessor is a technology that has been introduced into many new product configurations. Such introductions have changed the competitive factors and differentiated products, thus influencing markets significantly.

- Microprocessors control the fuel consumption of automobiles, directly resulting in a new competitive element of "better gas mileage."
- Microprocessors in microwave ovens allow the user to pop in a frozen mass at 8:00 A.M. and arrive home at 5:00 P.M. to a prepared meal.
- A microprocessor plays games with the kids, teaches French to a teenager, and balances the checkbook. It will even let Mom or Dad do the family tax return for the year.
- The microprocessor tucked neatly away in the thermostat in the hall can control the heat and air conditioning in the house, taking advantage of time-of-day utility rates, outside climate, and day and night differentials.

- A microprocessor in the home or office security system can detect fire, intrusions, and threats to security while informing the appropriate agency of the condition.

Microprocessors have almost limitless applications to existing products. These applications of existing technologies present a lower risk than the introduction of a new technology because both the existing technology and the existing product have established market acceptance.

It is also important to forecast for technological innovation and application. This factor can bring about product obsolescence and decreased marketability faster than almost any other influence.

A final major consideration concerning technology changes may be reflected in psychographic marketing factors.

- What benefits do your customers derive from using your product? What projected benefits do you anticipate adding and when?
- What adjectives do your customers use in describing your product, and what adjectives do you want them to apply?
- Whose endorsements will help promote sales of the product as configured in the future?
- Where are the products currently purchased, and how will that change with a change in technology?

The answers to these questions may indicate a product configuration for an electronic wristwatch that also has an alarm, night-light, stopwatch, waterproof case, calendar, and day/date functions. Advertising and marketing can be planned for many different approaches and markets based on the psychographic ("hot button") factors indicated.

The business should take two points into consideration with regard to governments.

1. What new governmental regulations may affect the way you currently do business?
2. What continuing and future regulations can be anticipated to have an impact on your business?

No business is immune from governmental regulation. Typical interventions include:

1. Product safety.
2. Licensure (certification).
3. Taxation.
4. Employee considerations:
   • Occupational Safety and Health Administration (OSHA)
   • Social Security
   • Unemployment compensation
   • Insurance
   • Pensions and other benefits
5. Regulation of output.
6. Price controls.
7. Import/export quotas and regulations.
8. Operating authority (permits).
9. Duties (import) and inspection.

Each of these (and other) categories has an associated cost, and in some cases established future requirements. For example, in the case of employee Social Security benefits, rate increases and ceilings have been established for future periods. These, of course, affect costs and therefore future product pricing. Each must be forecast for the planning horizon.

Whereas some governmental impacts may be predicted with reasonable accuracy, others, such as the currency exchange rate, may create serious problems. The results of governmental activity are not easily projected and even experts have difficulty in predicting governmental behavior, not to mention the impacts of that behavior. However, a reasonable attempt is better than no attempt.

Application of Forecasting Methods

Beginning in the 1920s, government and, later, private companies began compiling data and conducting quantitative analysis of the national economy. The intent of the studies was to devise a system that would signal changes in the business environment, warn of downturns, and predict the end of recessions. From the data collected, monthly, quarterly, and annual series on prices, employment, and production were generated as indicators of business health.

A number of data series, such as employment, indexes of consumer and wholesale prices, and manufacturers' orders are published in the nation's newspapers. These indicators are followed closely by many professionals, especially during periods of change in business activities.

Economic indicators have been grouped into three types: leading, coincidental, and lagging.

- *Leading.* These indicators provide advance warning of possible changes in business activities.
- *Coincidental.* These reflect the current performance of the economy.
- *Lagging.* These confirm a change previously signaled in the economic business activity.

Coincidental indicators are perhaps the most common and familiar. They include (for some products or services, these may also be leading or lagging indicators):

- Gross National Product.
- Industrial production.
- Personal income.
- Retail sales.
- Employment.

Whereas coincidental indicators are used to determine whether the economy is currently experiencing contraction, expansion, or stability, leading indicators are necessary for forecasting. Leading indicators help forecasters assess short-term trends in the coincidental indicators. In addition, leading indicators help planners and policy makers anticipate changes in the economy: They may indicate upturns or downturns in business. Anticipating downturns helps the business take corrective action and plan for the tightening of economic conditions. In the event that an upturn is suggested, the business could prepare to take advantage of the improvement in business conditions.

Housing starts is a key leading indicator for economic activity in some industries. Others include:

- New orders for durable goods.
- Construction contracts.
- Formation of new business enterprises.
- Hiring rates.
- Average length of workweek.

Using indicators for forecasting has been refined and developed by professional forecasting businesses that use sophisticated mathematical and statistical models to generate projections. For many smaller businesses, a manual algorithm, or a step-by-step approach, can produce effective projections. It is set out in the following steps:

1. Plot a time series of the industry's historical experience (sales per year, units per month, etc.).
2. Remove any seasonality by using some averaging or smoothing method. (Irregularities due to some obviously unusual problem such as a war may also require adjustment.)
3. Fit a trend using linear regression (least squares) or the eyeball method.
4. Repeat these steps for national, regional, local, or industrial or trade association data of a causal nature. For example, sales of replacement auto parts is related to sales of new autos in previous periods. The intent here is to find a comparative series.
5. If there is a historical relationship in the cycle pattern between that which you want to predict (sales of replacement parts) and the other data (sales of new cars), (a) obtain forecasts of the other variable(s), and (b) forecast the cycle for your variable based on the cycle for the economic variable.
6. Project the trend line determined in step 3 and add the cycle generated in step 5.

7. Remember the seasonal variations you may have attempted earlier to remove for simplicity.
8. Test the projection for reasonableness.

One of your concerns may be which indicators will be most relevant for comparative purposes. As mentioned throughout this book, trade association data and information are often most relevant and comparable. It is usually most appropriate for market share and market size determinations.

Comparative indicators can come from evaluation of demographic information about your product. By answering the following questions, you may be able to generate forecasts based on the growth patterns of these factors.

- What particular age group purchases your products?
- Are your products purchased by a specific ethnic group?
- Is your product purchased more frequently by either gender?
- Is the product geographically restricted?
- Are the products purchased by people of a particular income level?
- Are sales of the product tied to the sales of other products?
- Are the sales related to any one occupational category?
- What is the educational level of purchasers of the product?
- Who (according to the above categories) are the heaviest users of your product?

One method for testing the reasonableness of your forecasts is the use of scenarios. The use of scenarios offers you a technique designed to help you face the possible unpleasant situations that may occur.

A scenario is a story about the future that uses current facts and trends. The conclusion to the story is presented in a form that is easy to understand. It is important to remember that in scenario preparation, evaluation of the possible outcome initially has to be suspended so that discussion of the problem can occur objectively. Prejudging a scenario has a chilling effect on brainstorming. It is through creative brainstorming—always to be encouraged—that scenarios are created.

Summary

Forecasting is a combination of science and intuition, or, if you will, art. Its objective should be the generation of multiple forecasts based upon different scenarios. Getting involved in scenario generation helps managers steer clear of thinking there is only one way to run the business. It allows for creative, alternative planning.

The necessary analysis of the market, competitors, the economy, and the firm itself enlightens management as to the position of the firm in the market and price structure; how demand works; how the economic cycle affects the business plans; and how the firm can integrate these elements to forecast for better planning.

Appendix: Linear Regression

The term "linear regression" often scares people off. The more familiar expression, "least squares estimate," a form of linear regression, is less frightening and most people have been exposed to it. Many inexpensive calculators will make linear regression determinations after entry of the data.

Linear regression determines the placement of a line that minimizes the sum of the squares of the deviations of the actual data points from the straight line of best fit. The linear equation of the form

$$Y = MX + B$$

is determined for the line. *M* is the slope of the line, and *B* is the *Y* intercept. If the relationship is set up so that the cost of production is the *Y* axis and the units of production are the *X* axis, the *Y* intercept (the point of zero production), should approximate the fixed costs. In this model, the slope, *M*, is the change associated with an incremental change in production. This would indicate the variable cost. As the mathematics are somewhat complicated, we have developed the following worksheet (Figure 2.1) to ease the operation.

Some example data to fill in Figure 2.1 follows:

Assume for a given 12-month period the following data:

Month	Units	Costs
Jan	500	1,200
Feb	200	700
Mar	300	1,100
Apr	600	1,500
May	100	600
June	400	1,100
July	500	1,500
Aug	200	500
Sept	400	1,000
Oct	450	1,200
Nov	300	800
Dec	550	1,700
Total	4,500	12,900

FIGURE 2.1

Least Squares Line of Regression

Period	Column 1 Units	Column 2 Total Costs	Column 3 Col. 1 Squared	Column 4 Col. 1 × Col. 2
1				
2				
3				
4				
5				
6				
7				
8				
9				
10				
11				
12				
13				
14				
15				
TOTAL				

With this data, we can now use the form "Least Squares Line of Regression" to calculate the slope/intercept form of the equation of the "best-fit" line. Instructions for use of the form follow.

Instructions

(A) For each period, enter units produced in column 1 and costs in column 2.

(B) Square each figure in column 1 and enter the result in column 3.

(C) Multiply each figure in column 1 by the corresponding figure in column 2 and enter the product in column 4.

(D) Sum columns 1 through 4. Also determine the number of periods used.

(E) Now substitute the values obtained into the following two equations:

(1) Sum of column 2 = (number of periods) (a)
  + (sum of column 1) (b).
(2) Sum of column 4 = (sum of column 1) (a)
  + (sum of column 3) (b).

(F) To get (b), multiply equation 1 by (sum of column 1)/(number of periods) to produce equation 3. Subtract equation 3 from equation 2 and solve for (b).

(G) To get (a), substitute (b) above into either equation 1 or 2 and solve for (a).

(H) The figures thus obtained are used to construct the graph as follows:

a = the cost at zero units of production
b = the additional cost incurred with each unit of production

The example data have been placed into Figure 1 format. Column 1 contains production quantities and column 2 contains costs incurred. Let's assume that the periods are months so that we can ignore inflation and avoid adjusting the cost for it. This takes care of step (A).

Columns 3 and 4 have been filled in from steps (B) and (C). Totals are figured as called for in step (D) and the number of periods is 12. Figure 2.2 represents this information.

The equations in step (D) are:

$$(1) \; 12,900 = 12a + 4,500b \text{ and}$$
$$(2) \; 5,435,000 = 4,500a + 1,955,000b.$$

In step (F), we multiply equation (1) by 4,500/12, or 375, and get equation (3):

$$(3) \; 4,837,500 = 4500a + 1,687,500b$$

Subtracting equation (3) from equation (2) we get:

$$
\begin{array}{lll}
5,435,000 = & 4,500a + & 1,955,000b \\
\underline{4,837,000 = } & \underline{4,500a + } & \underline{1,687,500b} \\
598,000 = & & 267,500b \text{ and } b = 2.236
\end{array}
$$

In step (G) we substitute this value for (b) into either equation and find (a). Using equation (1):

$$12,900 = 12a + 4,500 \,(2.236)$$
$$a = 236.5$$

The resulting graph is shown as Figure 2.3.

The graph is constructed as follows:

(A) Find the point at which the line will cross the vertical axis. This is (a) or 236.5. Because it crosses the vertical axis at zero units of production we can use this as an approximation of fixed costs. Mark this point on the graph.

(B) Compute another point on the line. Take an arbitrary level of production such as 700 units and multiply this number by (b). This gives an approximation of variable costs. Add fixed costs to this figure. Example: (700) (2.236) + 236.5 = 1802. This figure will be the total costs of production at that level of production. Plot this point on the graph. Connect the two points.

FIGURE 2.2

Least Squares Line of Regression

Period	Column 1 Units	Column 2 Total Costs	Column 3 Col. 1 Squared	Column 4 Col. 1 × Col. 2
1	500	1,200	250,000	600,000
2	200	700	40,000	140,000
3	300	1,100	90,000	330,000
4	600	1,500	360,000	900,000
5	100	600	10,000	60,000
6	400	1,100	160,000	440,000
7	500	1,500	250,000	750,000
8	200	500	40,000	100,000
9	400	1,000	160,000	400,000
10	450	1,200	202,500	540,000
11	300	800	90,000	240,000
12	550	1,700	302,500	935,000
13				
14				
15				
Total	4,500	12,900	1,955,000	5,435,000

FIGURE 2.3

Cost of Production

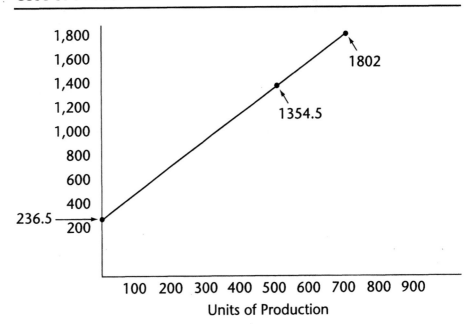

Operating the Business

Chapter 3

Marketing Analysis

This chapter will discuss the use of the well-known product matrix analysis. We will show how this may be used to assist in planning both the marketing and manufacturing strategies. We will also examine how to analyze marketing costs and will provide an outline for a marketing-oriented cost accounting system. We will cover the nature, behavior, and assignment of marketing costs and their relationship to contribution margin accounting. A section will be devoted to correcting product weaknesses in the market and another to segmenting markets. We will examine the channels used for the distribution of products, how to handle changes, and how to improve distribution either through existing channels or by seeking new channels. Finally, we will give a checklist of questions to be asked in order to establish how well your marketing plan is meeting your business objectives.

Product Matrix Analysis

Very often, a company carries lines of similar and even competing products. For a retail business, this may cause inventory control problems and additional costs associated with storage, ordering, and handling. Questions arise as to which products to continue or discontinue and where new lines or products may need to be added.

One method of using the product matrix analysis is a two-variable matrix analysis. Each product the firm sells may be evaluated in this method. It is a simple analytical tool for determining the constituent parts of each product's market. On a square matrix, quality or any variable of interest is plotted across the bottom from low quality on the left to high quality on the right. Going down the side, a price scale is made, from high on the top to low on the bottom. Fair value would be along the diagonal. Figure 3.1 is an example of this tool.

Then, using a separate graph for each of the firm's products, the marketing department can establish where each product is on the graph. If the product is priced fairly, for the quality it represents, it should be somewhere on the diagonal.

As an example, assume that Shirts, Inc., a manufacturer of casual shirts for men, is a solid brand carried by several large chain department stores. Also within the market are three old, established brands (O1, O2, O3) and two designer brands (D1, D2). The company first plots where it believes its product fits in the quality/price matrix and then plots where the other businesses appear to be. Figure 3.2 depicts what the market for men's casual shirts looks like for the business.

Shirts, Inc. and firms O1 and O2 have priced their products competitively, based on the value analysis. They are giving fair value to the consumer, pricing their goods in accordance with quality. Firms D1 and D2 are selling shirts at prices higher than the quality dictates, meaning that something other than quality (label, prestige, advertising, etc.) is driving the market.

Firm O3, however, is selling high-quality goods at a price less than fair value. This should be a warning sign. Firm O3 may be trying to cut into the other firms' existing market share; they may have a bad pricing policy; or they may be trying to increase sales because of financial problems. For whatever reason, firm O3 should be monitored as a potentially dangerous competitor in this situation.

This analysis does have some limitations:

- It assumes knowledgeable matrix users who analyze the price/ quality relationship.
- It does not consider other extrinsic motivating factors: name recognition, fashion, styles, fads, and so on.
- It assumes comparable products.

Figure 3.1

Value Grid

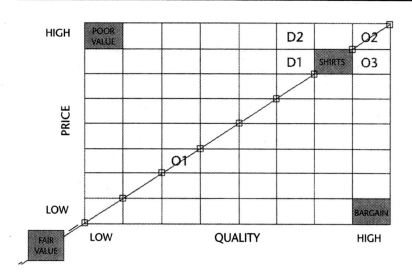

Figure 3.2

Value Grid

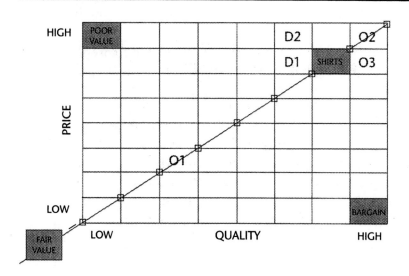

Another interesting outcome of this analysis is that it points out that the firm selling a low-price, low-quality product is still selling a fair-value product for which there may be a market. If gaps in the market are evident, one could produce a different "value" product to meet these market opportunities.

For example, for a particular product line, one could produce and price a shirt for each level of quality along the diagonal. In this manner, it would blanket the market. Competition might then be forced to focus on those other extrinsic factors that differentiate their products.

Each of a company's products can be evaluated in this manner. Also, other variables could be placed on the bottom axis (prestige, sex appeal, image, etc.), with various conclusions to be drawn. Additionally, complementary products can be placed on the same grid to analyze any linkage between the sales of each. Conceptually, this analysis can be extended to three dimensions (price, quality, and image), but that is very difficult to visualize and to depict.

Unit Product Contribution Analysis

In looking at the aggregate product line versus the price–quality relationship, more information may be needed to evaluate the effectiveness of product mix. Cost and contribution provides the necessary data. Consider the unit product contribution analysis sheet shown as Figure 3.3.

When the necessary data are compiled to prepare this spreadsheet, it becomes apparent which products make a contribution to overall fixed costs and which do not (Figure 3.4).

The performance of Product B2 should be of concern to the firm, as it does not sustain its directly attributable costs (or make any contribution to the corporate fixed expenses).

Carrying the analysis further to demonstrate contribution as a percentage of price can also be a helpful exercise. The matrix can quickly point out where attention should be concentrated. Other types of comparisons can be generated by grouping product lines together and evaluating the comparative contributions between lines (Figure 3.5).

One other factor may be introduced into the analysis: the existing and projected sales levels. A company may not produce enough

FIGURE 3.3

Unit Product Contribution Analysis (by Unit)

| PRODUCTS | NET SELLING PRICE | COSTS | | | | | CONTRIBUTION PER UNIT | PERCENT CONTRIBUTION |
		MATERIAL	LABOR	VARIABLE OVERHEAD	OTHER	TOTAL		
LINE A								
A1								
A2								
A3								
LINE B								
B1								
B2								
B3								

FIGURE 3.4

Unit Product Contribution Analysis (by Unit)

| PRODUCTS | NET SELLING PRICE | COSTS | | | | | CONTRIBUTION PER UNIT | PERCENT CONTRIBUTION |
		MATERIAL	LABOR	VARIABLE OVERHEAD	OTHER	TOTAL		
LINE A								
A1	$5.47	$1.35	$2.01	$0.17	$0.00	$3.53	$1.94	35.47%
A2	$6.15	$1.39	$2.10	$0.19	$0.00	$3.68	$2.47	40.16%
A3	$6.27	$1.20	$2.15	$0.20	$0.05	$3.60	$2.67	42.58%
LINE B								
B1	$7.99	$2.10	$1.75	$0.16	$0.07	$4.08	$3.91	48.94%
B2	$8.99	$3.27	$4.97	$0.30	$0.50	$9.04	($0.05)	-0.56%
B3	$9.99	$3.15	$3.10	$0.27	$0.00	$6.52	$3.47	34.73%
B4	$10.50	$4.00	$2.97	$0.39	$0.00	$7.36	$3.14	29.90%

Figure 3.5

Product and Product Line Contribution Analysis

| | PRODUCT LINE A | | | | PRODUCT LINE B | | | | | GRAND TOTAL |
	1	2	3	TOTAL	1	2	3	4	TOTAL	
UNIT CONTRIBUTION										
BY %	36.00%	40.00%	43.00%		49.00%	0.00%	35.00%	30.00%		
BY $	$1.94	$2.47	$2.67		$3.91	($0.05)	$3.47	$3.14		
BY VOLUME	10,000	25,000	27,000		8,000	2,000	21,000	37,000		
TOTAL										
CONTRIBUTION	$19,400	$61,750	$72,090	$153,240	$31,280	($100)	$72,870	$116,180	$220,230	$373,470

FIGURE 3.6

Customer Sales Anticipation

CUSTOMER _____   SALESPERSON _____

	1 QUARTER	2 QUARTER	3 QUARTER	4 QUARTER	YEAR
PRODUCT LINE A					
PRODUCT A1					
PRODUCT A2					
PRODUCT A3					
PRODUCT A4					
PRODUCT LINE B					
PRODUCT B1					
PRODUCT B2					
PRODUCT B3					
PRODUCT B4					

of certain products in its line to have a significant cost or profit effect. However, in order to be competitive, the company may need these products to have a "complete line" and to service its customers.

One should consider sales forecasting with an eye on the percentage contribution each line and each type within each line gives to the bottom line. The next logical step in the process is to project sales by product line and type.

There are two sources of sales forecasting: internally generated numbers and customer-generated projections. Sometimes, internally generated numbers are produced by people who do not know the market. It is better to have the customer-contact people—the salespeople—generate these data.

FIGURE 3.7

Customer Sales and Call Plan

CUSTOMER NAME	CUSTOMER CATEGORY	EXISTING (E) NEW (N)	PRIOR YEAR'S SALES	PROJECTED SALES	CALL PLAN
		EXISTING			
		NEW			

A format such as that in Figure 3.6 can be very helpful in getting the salespeople to think at the level of the specific customer, specific product, and specific time frame. This detailed information is very beneficial for planning purposes.

In order to compile projected sales information from customers in a uniform and consistent manner, the survey form shown in Figure 3.7 can be used to solicit estimates from customers as salespeople visit with them.

As the salespeople call on customers, they can be polled concerning their expectations for sales of your products. Obviously, the more details addressed (specific products, colors, time, etc.) the better. From this information, the salespeople can produce their call plan for getting back to the customer on a timely basis.

By using the above outline approach to product matrix analysis, one can generate useful information displayed in an easily recognizable manner. The process is another tool available for the quantification and comparison of a marketing program.

Analyzing the Impact of Marketing Dollars

In order to maximize the utility of marketing dollars, it is important to establish quantified objectives for each marketing program and carefully monitor the results of those programs. The programs should embody significant feedback loops to allow for the modification of the marketing plan in the event it fails to be effective.

Analyzing Marketing Costs

The foundation essential to success in monitoring marketing plans is a good system for identifying and assigning costs. Such foundation permits you to pinpoint wasted effort and ineffective programs. The real problem lies in the fact that many owner-managers do not have the necessary information to begin to make an analysis. Is that information not available?

Typical accounting systems, following generally accepted accounting procedures, may be oriented toward external reporting and not toward sales or marketing decision making. Such systems frequently lump all marketing costs into one or a handful of "selling expenses." The categories often used by accountants may be too broad for useful analysis of sales and marketing considerations.

Often, accountants have not been adequately educated to appreciate the nature of all the various marketing elements, components, and costs. Accountants, therefore, may concern themselves chiefly with getting all marketing costs assigned somewhere—often with little regard for the appropriateness of those assignments or the behavior of the costs.

Many owners of small businesses fail to establish marketing programs with the care used to establish other objectives. Often marketing programs are established on the basis of tradition, industry practices, or rules of thumb. Frequently, small companies try to match a competitor's sales force on a one-to-one basis, instead of setting clear, measurable objectives for marketing endeavors.

What you need, then, is to establish a marketing-oriented, cost accounting system, with the proper assignment and allocation of marketing costs, as well as a working understanding of the behavior of these costs. Finally, you should establish a formal program of marketing objectives with the obvious "results management" follow-up. This would also require the necessary feedback loop to ensure that marketing programs do not operate without close supervision and control.

Checklist for a Marketing-Oriented Cost Accounting System

A reasonable chart of accounts for sales and marketing should address the following:

1. *Salaries and commissions*
   - Sales representatives
   - Marketing management and administration
   - Sales management
   - Marketing communications
   - Shipping
   - Credit and collections
   - Market research
   - Order processing
2. *Marketing communications*
   - Advertising
   - Sales promotion
   - Merchandising
   - Publicity
   - Trade shows and exhibits
   - Direct mail
   - Samples

- Literature
- Telephone expenses
- Package design

3. *Shipping*
   - Materials
   - Freight
   - Depreciation

4. *Customer service*
   - Entry of orders
   - Order processing
   - Billing
   - Telephone expenses

5. *Other marketing costs*
   - Finished goods inventory, inventory carrying discounts and markdowns
   - Marketing research
   - Sales office
   - Returns
   - Travel and entertainment
   - Credit and collections
   - Refunds
   - Warranties

The preceding checklist is not intended to be an exclusive marketing-oriented cost accounting system. Such a system must be tailored to your specific needs. There may be other elements not on this list that should be considered in setting up the system. The objective should be to establish a marketing-oriented accounting system that permits an analysis of marketing costs and results in some detail. The marketing accounting system should also be capable of providing cost analysis on the basis of the following categories:

- Market or market segment
- Channel of distribution
- Product and product line
- Geographic region, distribution center, or sales territory
- Account type and individual accounts

You may not feel the need for this level of sophistication. However, if you generate this information, the analysis can show you what costs, other than sales and advertising, are being incurred and the results of these costs.

Nature, Behavior, or Assignment of Costs

Marketing costs do not fundamentally differ from other types of business costs; they can be broadly classified as either fixed or variable.

Variable costs are those that vary in relation to the amount or frequency of an activity or function. Some marketing costs that may typically be classified as variable include trade discounts, cash discounts, freight charges, and sales commission.

Fixed costs are those that do not vary in the amount of product manufactured or sold. Typically such costs include district sales managers' salaries, base salaries for sales representatives, and cost of operating regional sales offices.

In addition, there are other fixed, general expenses that usually are treated as overhead. Such costs may include salaries of chief operating officers and administrative staff, the cost of operating electronic data processing systems, the cost of maintaining the company's headquarters, insurance, property taxes, and so on.

Contribution Accounting

In essence, contribution accounting answers the question of how much money a particular unit contributes in excess of certain agreed costs to meet the continuing demands of carrying general overhead. To measure contribution to fixed expenses of a particular product, a four-step procedure is undertaken:

1. Calculate the income generated for that product.
2. Subtract the variable portion of direct labor, direct material, and any variable overhead associated with that product, at that production level.
3. Subtract other variable costs, such as commissions, freight, and the like.

4. Finally, subtract the total program cost incurred solely for that product (this is a little more difficult to identify, but such costs as product advertising will fall into this category).

When you have concluded this four-step evaluation, you are left with the amount available for contribution to the company's general expenses, which may also be calculated as a percentage, by dividing the contribution by the income generated in step one. Such a number is quite useful in determining a product or product line's overall effectiveness.

Continuing Programs

Even marketing programs that appear to be working effectively should be assessed periodically to guard against a decline in effectiveness. Continuous measuring of programs usually results in better program control. Complacency is one of the biggest dangers to marketing effectiveness.

Keeping products and services aimed at customers and prospective customers is a delicate combination of looking forward for trends and looking back at an analysis of accomplishments and failures. Examine present and past records to determine weaknesses and strengths in the market. Also, look ahead and plan for the necessary changes to correct weaknesses and exploit strengths.

Correcting Weaknesses

One method of correcting weaknesses is to look at the firm's product matrix and determine which items are slow movers versus those that may be up-and-comers. A second correction may come from looking to the margin available to retailers and wholesalers. A different, more liberal policy here may encourage pushing the firm's products over those of its competitors.

In a highly competitive market, smaller segments of that market may be targeted and efforts concentrated in those areas to improve marketing potentials. An example would be support hose for ladies, an attractive submarket of the overall hosiery market. Looking for an opportunity to target a specialized product in a segment of a general market is often rewarding. It is noteworthy that both the opportunity and associated costs in segmenting a market have to be considered. There are identifiable expenses associated with product differentiation. Advertising must be specialized and directed at the target market. Manufacturing may incur additional costs to handle the special materials used in a specialized product. Different packaging may be required.

Established products can drift off target when a substitute product, with more appeal to the consumer, appears in that market. One may need to look to those elements that make the competing product more attractive to customers: price, convenience, novelty, and so on. If the adverse trend cannot be reversed, a viable alternative may be to find a substitute use for the product rather than abandoning the product. Look at the growth in use of shock absorber–type products. They are now used for automobile rear hatch openers, rowing machines, and other weight-lifting and exercise equipment.

Examining Channels

Marketing channels may also be potential areas of weakness for small manufacturers. Distribution channels can lose their effectiveness for many reasons. Consumer buying habits many change, competition may develop, different cost incentives cause the channels to shift emphasis, or the company may simply develop alternative objectives. Therefore, channels should be reviewed periodically to see that they are in fact performing effectively and consistently with your objectives.

Checklist for Channel Review

Determine whether the channels are a means to an end by asking such questions as:

- Who buys my product?
- Where do they buy it?

- How do they buy it—by single lots or by the dozen?
- How frequently do they buy it?
- Are my ultimate users satisfied in buying through present channels?

Sources of Market Information

Examine the following:

- Warranty return cards
- Information provided by distributors
- Trade associations
- Trade journals
- Government publications

Improving Channels

Some helpful hints in improving marketing channels include the following:

- Actively seek cooperation with resellers who have active feedback opportunities. It is through such cooperation that resellers can increase their effectiveness in moving product.
- Provide resellers with selling tools such as counter cards, displays, and other helpful promotional information.
- Better cooperation may be obtained by providing distributors with technical aid and help in inventory control.
- Monitor resellers' margins available from competitors and, if necessary, take corrective action to keep your products competitive in the eyes of the seller.
- Finally, it may be necessary to seek new channels when present channels become ineffective.

Creative planning may offer alternatives and new methods of channeling your product to the ultimate consumer. For example:

- Paperback book manufacturers found that magazine wholesalers could provide mass distribution to newsstands, drugstores, and supermarkets.

- Producers of inexpensive throwaway pens found that distribution through tobacco wholesalers got the pens into many small stores.
- Sometimes, as a manufacturer, you may have to set up your own organization to overcome such problems. It should be noted, however, that such action can be exceptionally costly.

Normally, changing distribution channels is not without additional costs. Old, established relationships may have to be broken, and moving into new channels may interfere with relationships already existing in those channels.

In some cases, it may be necessary to change your entire business image to compensate for changing marketing strategies. For example, a drug company refused to sell its drugs through discount houses. Ultimately, it had to modify its business decision and compromise to the extent that it would sell through discount houses in which there were licensed pharmacists. In this way, the firm increased the exposure for its product but maintained a more exclusive image.

Seven Points to Assist in the Definition of Your Business

In order to market products effectively, there are many things management should know. Some information is easily obtained; other information is difficult and expensive. The following questions may be of value in determining what you know.

1. List your five major classes of customers.
   - What are the common characteristics of those customers?
   - Why do they buy your product? Be *very* specific.
2. Analyze each product or product line in terms of:
   - Revenue
   - Percent of total revenue
   - Profit and percent of total profit
3. List three potential customers who do not currently do business with you. *Why* don't they do business with you?
4. List five adjectives your customers use to describe the business or product. What do these words mean to you?
5. Is there any obvious ethnic, age, religious, gender, or other majority in the firm's customer base?

6. What is the most effective sales outlet?
7. If customers could not buy what you sell (even from a competitor) what would they do? This last question has some profound significance in determining how your product is perceived in the market (as luxury, necessity, etc). A well-reasoned answer will reveal the need the product meets and might also indicate alternate ways to meet that need.

Fourteen Questions to Assist in the Definition of the Market

Knowing what need you meet (or could meet) leads to the question of who has that need and what prompts them to buy. The following questions can assist you in focusing in on your market.

Demographics

1. Are products purchased primarily by any particular age group?
2. Are products purchased by any specific ethnic group?
3. Are products purchased by one gender?
4. Are products purchased primarily within any one geographic area?
5. Are products purchased by any income level group?
6. Are sales of products tied to sales or use of other products?
7. Are sales of products tied largely to any occupational category?
8. What is the education level of the primary purchasers?
9. Who, according to the above categories, is the heaviest user of the product?

Psychographics

10. List the benefits each class of customer derives from using the product. Be *very* specific.
11. List the adjectives customers use to describe your product.
12. Which advertising has been most effective?
13. Whose endorsements might cause a person to buy the product?
14. Where are the products primarily purchased (type of store, channels of distribution, etc.)?

Demographics and psychographics are two useful approaches to gathering data to determine the characteristics and attitudes of buyers. Demographics specify groups by age, sex, income, marital status, education, and geography. It then correlates buying responses with those characteristics. Psychographics deal with buying patterns motivated by attitudes rather than external characteristics. Psychographics chart personality, values, and interests.

Assessing the Competition

As important as it is to assess your own products and marketing processes, it is at least equally important to do a thorough analysis of the competition. Sometimes this is relatively easy and does not need to be sophisticated; sometimes it requires a great deal of research and expertise. Much of what needs to be done was referenced in Chapter 1. We will refer to a number of forms and concepts already dealt with in that material.

The strategic factors analysis (Figure 1.5) and the related suggestions for use (Figure 1.6) can be very effectively used in the competitive assessment. Finding out who the competitors are, what their strengths and weaknesses are, and what you believe their most immediate moves might be will be very revealing. Then, a strategic plan of action (Figure 1.7) will provide specific steps to be taken relative to those competitors.

Information developed in the formulation of the salesperson's sales forecast (by customer) (Figure 1.9) and the sales forecast summary (Figure 1.10) can produce interesting field-based perceptions of what the competition is doing and what responses are appropriate.

Another interesting and revealing approach is to apply the thirty questions to assist with strategic planning (Appendix D of Chapter 1) to your competitors. You may find it is even more difficult to answer these questions about your competitors than it is to answer them about yourself. However, the process of asking the questions and trying to determine the answers, particularly as you involve more people from your organization, will be an excellent competitive analysis.

You may also want to try to apply the internal data monitoring (Appendix E of Chapter 1) to various competitors. The more information you are able to develop about how they conduct business, where they make their money, and why, the better able you will be to devise plans to improve your ability to compete. In fact, almost any of the planning tools presented in Chapter 1 can be used as competitor assessment tools as well.

Reverse engineering of products and services is a valuable tool. The process is more obvious with tangible products than with intangible services, so we will discuss products. However, it is applicable to services as well and is very helpful when so applied.

Reverse engineering of products requires you to acquire the product and to take it apart, noting every detail of its design and composition. It is an attempt to determine exactly how the product is made, what all of the components are, and why the competitor chooses to do it that way. From this you may determine a number of changes to your process that will be cost saving and/or improvements to quality.

Summary

One of the initial concerns for the firm is the nature of the market, the competitors present in the market, and the availability of competitive products. This can be quickly visualized using a product matrix analysis. On the market grid, your products are located according to an analysis of the quality and price or other appropriate relationships. These relationships are based on the assumption, for example, that demand reacts to the perception that a product's price accurately reflects the value of that product. If it does not, that too indicates an important market fact about the product or the firm. For example, if the product is selling at a price above that warranted by the quality, other factors are causing this market acceptance. This is typical for designer clothes. They are generally priced—and do, in fact, sell—above the price normally dictated for their quality. The factor driving this "price premium" is fashion or prestige. Extrinsic variables often affect the pricing policies of the firm.

Analysis of your product lines using a contribution margin analysis will indicate the financial strengths and weaknesses of your product distribution. To this you can add an analysis of the impact of your marketing dollars on sales. In doing these analyses, it may become apparent that your accounting and control systems do not account well for the marketing function. Accountants are generally concerned with fitting costs into appropriate categories and often lump all marketing costs into one or two accounts. This is probably inadequate to serve as a basis for proper marketing analysis. As part of the existing accounting system, an accounting subsystem can be developed to provide the necessary cost information for marketing decision making.

Chapter 4

Pricing

Pricing the product or service of the company can be quite simple. Someone simply establishes a price—cost-based, volume-based, market-based, or without a basis. The trick for success is to price so that the product or service will be purchased *and* the company can make a profit.

An acceptable price usually falls within the bounds of a "price ceiling" and a "price floor." The market generally determines the price under which products will sell and thus establishes a price ceiling. Costs and desired profits establish a price floor below which one cannot sell and make the desired profit. Pricing practices often get out of date as a result of rising costs, material shortages, wide swings in economy, difficult access to funds for expansion and operation, and tougher competition at home and from abroad. Good pricing practices require an understanding of the influences of market factors: the economy, technology, competition, and the competing pressures on limited resources. In addition to these factors, you must constantly consider those related to internally generated costs.

Basic Rules of Pricing

Good pricing practices generally recognize that there is more to pricing than consideration of only internal costs. Two important factors in developing prices for small companies are:

1. Recognition that the market, not your costs, determines the price at which the product will sell.
2. An awareness that your costs and desired profits establish only a price floor below which you cannot sell and still make a profit.

The area between the price ceiling, established by the market, and the price floor, determined by cost and desired profit, is one view of the "relevant price range" often discussed but seldom defined in textbooks. It is only when a business can produce at a cost that will permit recovery of those costs plus a desired profit margin that the price determined by the market will sustain the business in a profitable mode.

Cost as a Factor

Without good cost information, any pricing policy is inadequate at best. Good cost data are as important for pricing as they are for operational management of the business. If you do not have adequate cost figures, you should require the accounting department to develop them for use both in operations control and for the necessary pricing decisions.

Methods of Pricing Using Cost as a Basis

There are several methods of establishing price floors using your costs. Each has advantages and disadvantages.

- *Markup on cost method.* Among nonmanufacturers the simplest, and a frequently used, method for developing price floors is markup on cost of goods. This generally involves adding a percentage to the cost of goods. This markup is intended to cover all other costs and the necessary profit levels for the business. Keystoning (doubling the invoice cost) is an example of this method.
- *Full cost basis.* This method has been designed to recover all costs plus a margin. It is calculated by developing the total cost for manufacturing the product and then adding a markup, or fraction, to those costs. The formula is:

$$P = TC + [M\% \times TC]$$

or, price equals the total cost per unit plus a mark-up as a percentage times the total cost. The advantage of this method is clearly its simplicity of application. The major disadvantage is that the methodology used for the allocation of overhead expenses (as a part of total cost) may create an artificial number.

- *Incremental cost basis.* Using this method, total cost is abandoned in favor of the use of direct labor and direct material costs as the basis for setting price. It emphasizes the incremental cost of producing additional units. In using this method, normally, a larger markup is required on a smaller base than in the full cost system mentioned above. The emphasis is shifted toward production that can absorb more overhead. The formula is:

$$P = (DL + DM) + [M\% \times (DL + DM)]$$
$$= [(1 + M\%) \times (DL + DM)]$$

or, price equals direct labor plus direct material plus a markup as a percentage, times the sum of direct labor plus direct materials. This method is often used to price special orders. In the longer term, one must be sure the markup is sufficient to cover both overhead and profit.

- *Conversion cost basis.* Conversion cost–based pricing emphasizes the value added, or the direct labor plus overhead (costs needed to convert materials into product), in developing a price floor. The formula for this method is:

$$P = (DL + OH) + [M\% \times (DL + OH)]$$
$$= [(1 + M\%) \times (DL + OH)]$$

or, price equals direct labor plus overhead plus a markup as a percentage times the sum of direct labor and overhead. A necessary condition of this system is that overhead allocation must be based on some clear rationale. For this reason, it offers the higher potential for errors in pricing.

Other Cost-Based Approaches

There are methods that have been designed to determine prices required to accomplish the firm's objectives, such as a specified or target margin or a return on investment objective.

Target Margin. If the objective is to establish a price that will return a specific margin on sales, the method is simply: price = total cost/(100% − PM%), where *PM* is the expected profit margin. This method clearly identifies a price at which we must sell in order to achieve a desired margin on sales.

Target Return on Investment. As in the profit margin example, this method determines a price that must be charged in order to achieve a desired rate of return on investment. The formula is:

$$P = \frac{\left[\left(ROI\right) \times \left(\frac{I}{2}\right)\right] + \left(\frac{I}{Y}\right) + FC + \left[\left(VC\right) \times O\right]}{Q}$$

or, price equals the targeted before tax return times the average investment, plus the amortized return of the investment plus, fixed costs, plus the variable costs per unit times the quantity sold, all divided by the quantity sold. The critical variable in the formula is an estimation of the quantity that will be sold. Often sales volumes are very sensitive to price. Marketing experts may have to vary their projections and estimates after recalculating the price. One gets caught in a chicken-and-egg problem here in that in determining the price, the quantity may vary, and making adjustments for the quantity may alter the price.

Take as an example Newtown Manufacturing Co, which has a new product and wishes to set the price. The accounting department has established the following costs:

Direct labor (DL)	$.20/unit
Direct materials (DM)	.25/unit
Overhead (OH)	.11/unit
Total cost	$.56/unit

It calculates the price using three of the pricing methods:

1. Full cost pricing with a 50 percent margin:

$$\begin{aligned}
\text{Price} &= TC + (M\%)(TC) \\
&= \$.56 + (50\%)(.56) \\
&= .56 + .28 \\
&= \$.84
\end{aligned}$$

2. Incremental cost pricing with a 100 percent margin:

$$\begin{aligned}
\text{Price} &= (DL + DM) + (M\%)(DL + DM) \\
&= (.20 + .25) + (1.00)(.20 + .25) \\
&= .45 + .45 \\
&= .90
\end{aligned}$$

3. Conversion cost pricing with a 200 percent margin:

$$\begin{aligned}
\text{Price} &= (DL + OH) + (M\%)(DL + OH) \\
&= (.20 + .11) + (2.00)(.20 + .11) \\
&= (.31) + 2.0(.31) \\
&= .31 + 62 \\
&= .93
\end{aligned}$$

Target Margin on Sales. The Newtown Manufacturing Co. believes it can get a 25 percent sales (gross profit) margin. The firm wants to calculate a price using a target margin on sales method. The formula is:

$$\text{Price} = \frac{\text{Total Cost per Unit}}{100\% - (PM\%)}$$

$$\text{Price} = \frac{.56}{1.00 - .25}$$

$$\text{Price} = \frac{.56}{.75} = \$.75$$

Target Return on Investment Pricing. The Newtown Manufacturing Co. has developed a new product that requires a substantial investment.

The company wants to be sure that it gets a satisfactory return. It requires a 30 percent (before taxes) return. It is in the 46 percent tax bracket. This will give the firm about a 16 percent after-tax return. The accountant estimates the following costs:

Investment required $2,000,000.00
Fixed costs $40,000.00
Variable cost/unit $2.50

The investment is targeted for repayment in five years, and the firm estimates sales at 100,000 units per year. Using the equation for target return on investment pricing, the following price is calculated:

$$\text{Price} = \frac{[(ROI) \times (I/2)] + (I/Y) + FC + [(VC) \times Q]}{Q}$$

$$\text{Price} = \frac{[.3 \times (2,000,000/2)] + [2,000,000/5] + 40,000 + [2.50 \times 100,000]}{100,000}$$

$$\text{Price} = \frac{[.3 \times 1,000,000] + [400,000] + 40,000 + 250,000}{100,000}$$

$$\text{Price} = \frac{300,000 + 400,000 + 40,000 + 250,000}{100,000}$$

$$\text{Price} = \frac{990,000}{100,000}$$

Price = $9.90

The "proof" of this price follows:

Annual sales $990,000
Less: Fixed costs   (40,000)
    Variable costs   (250,000)
    Straight-line depreciation (400,000)

Before-tax profit	300,000
Taxes at 46%	(138,000)
After-tax profit	$162,000

$$\text{Average investment} = (\$2,000,000/2) = \$1,000,000$$
$$\text{Before-tax return} = \$300,000/1,000,000 = 30\%$$
$$\text{After-tax return} = \$162,000/\$1,000,000 = 16.2\%$$

Target Costing

The problem with setting prices based on a target margin or return on investment is that it can be very difficult to determine the cost of a new product before it has reached the production process, at which point management may realize that the cost is so much higher than expectations that there is no way to reach targeted margin levels without charging a price that is vastly higher than that of competing products. To avoid this problem with unknown or runaway costs, one can implement a target costing system.

The concept behind target costing is simple—to first determine the price at which a company intends to sell a product, and then subtract a profit, which leaves the product cost that must be attained; if the engineering staff cannot create a product that sells for the targeted cost, then the company will not manufacture it. Though the concept is simple, this approach calls for an entirely different method for designing products. Rather than having the engineering team work in isolation from all other parts of the company while it creates new products, it must now be closely aligned with the marketing department, which scours the marketplace for information about new products and price points, and feeds this information back to the engineering staff, which uses it in concert with the marketing department to arrive at a series of conceptual designs for new products. The accounting staff is also involved, contributing to each new product the services of a cost accountant, who carefully researches the cost of each design during various stages of its development to ensure that it will reach its cost goal. The cost accountant is extremely valuable to the design effort, since the engineers gain rapid feedback regarding the cost of their designs, and modify the designs to meet cost goals.

In addition, a representative from the purchasing staff is involved, whose task is to source the parts included in product designs to determine the most likely part costs at various volume levels. This is an easier job if the engineering staff already has an approved library of parts used in other products, because the purchasing department has already lined up suppliers and determined prices for these parts. Finally, the manufacturing staff, usually represented by an industrial engineer, is added to the design team in order to determine the best way to produce a prospective product. There can be significant cost savings in this area that contribute greatly to attaining a product's target cost, because the industrial engineer can recognize whether a specific design will require an unusually expensive production layout, extra machinery, additional labor time, or perhaps may be subject to breakage, in which case scrap and warranty costs must also be added to the product cost. Clearly, the target costing approach requires the services of nearly every part of a company, but results in products with good margins that are easy to manufacture, and therefore are well worth the efforts of the additional personnel.

Most of a product's costs are designed into it. Once the design has been completed and released for production, there is little that the purchasing or production staffs can do to reduce a product's costs, because the bulk of the cost is in the parts used to make the product, and those are specified in the design. However, even an increase in costs of just a few percentage points subsequent to design completion can put a large dent in the level of expected profit, especially when the anticipated profit level was planned to be relatively low. Consequently, the cost accounting staff must remain watchful after a product design is complete, constantly comparing actual to budgeted costs, component by component, to ensure that purchased part costs are staying in line with expectations, not to mention similar tracking of in-house production costs.

When starting up a target costing project, the design team will allocate the total amount of allowed costs to all subsets of the product being designed. This is done so that the engineers assigned to each subset will have a budgeted cost that they must not exceed. This cost allocation can be done in several ways. One is to allocate costs based on the perceived value of each subset in contributing to the final product price. For example, the marketing staff may determine that the

Figure **4.1**

Target Costing Allocation Method

Sub-Sets of Treadmill Product

Description	Initial Cost	Percent of Initial Cost	Total Target Cost	Target Cost Allocation
Display Panel	$450	20%		$360
Motor	850	38%		684
Belt	325	15%		270
Platform	375	17%		306
Side Rails	215	10%		180
Totals	$2,215	100%	$1,800	$1,800

display panel on a $2,000 treadmill contributes $250 toward the product price, while the motor contributes $700 toward the price—each will be assigned those amounts, which they are not allowed to exceed when creating their subsets of the final product. The problem with this approach is that the assignment of cost budgets is partially based on the perceived value of parts of a product, which can be highly subjective. An alternative approach that is more factually based is to develop a preliminary costing analysis of all subsets of a product to determine their actual costs, prior to delving into ways to reduce them. One can then assign costs to each of the subsets in proportion to their initial costs, as is shown in Figure 4.1. In the example, we have broken down a treadmill into its major subsets and determined the preliminary cost of each one. We then determine each subset's preliminary proportion of the total product expense and assign a cost budget to it based on that percentage. This allocation method can also be skewed if the cost of some subsets can be quickly reduced through various means, such as lower supplier pricing or better internal manufacturing methods, while other subsets may be very difficult to reduce in cost. Accordingly, this budget allocation can be repeatedly recalculated, based on the revised costs of product sub-sets, resulting in new and more accurate cost allocations. In this manner, the various parts of a new product can be brought in line with expected costs.

Sometimes a product design cannot be completed at or below its designated cost budget. A large engineering team may labor for months to bring costs down to a targeted level, only to find that no more costs can be wrung out of it. The problem for a company that is paying for this large group of people to design the product is that it just paid the expenses for the entire project team, and now has no product to offset its initial investment. To avoid this problem, the engineering manager should schedule a series of review meetings, during which the design team must prove that it is gradually reducing costs down to the goal. For example, the project team must drive costs down to within 12 percent of the target cost within one month of project initiation, then to within 8 percent the next month, and so on. This approach tells management that progress is being made, and allows it to quickly "pull the plug" on any design project that is clearly unable to meet its costing goal.

One of the best ways to ensure that the cost of component parts stays low after production commences is to negotiate contracts with suppliers that lock in long-term part prices. Suppliers will agree to such contracts if they think there is a sufficient volume of future parts orders to justify the risk of not raising prices. Also, some companies will assume that future product prices will decline over time as a response to competitive pressures, and so will budget for *reductions* in part prices, which it will negotiate in advance from its suppliers. So, for example, the supplier of part will agree to a continuing series of six percent price declines, year after year, in a part it sells to a company. In order to achieve such declines, a company must be willing to send its engineering staff to supplier locations to help them wring costs out of their operations, and may also have to guarantee minimum order quantities to the suppliers. The cost accounting staff can also become involved in such a cost reduction plan, verifying the contractual dates on which suppliers have agreed to reduce their prices. This approach is well worth the effort, especially for products that sell in great volume, thereby adequately spreading the expense of cost monitoring and supplier negotiations over many units.

By using target costing, a company can ensure that its product prices will result in targeted margins. This is done by subjecting all product designs to a rigorous series of costing reviews during the design process, so that excessively expensive products are eliminated before they ever reach the production floor. Also, all products must be subject to ongoing reviews after production commences, to ensure that costing goals continue to be met. Only through this intensive review process can a company be assured that the profit margins it projects are the ones it actually attains.

Price Ceiling

The other half of the pricing concern is the price ceiling. The price ceiling is generally determined by the market and is often more difficult to estimate than the price floors. Many factors such as the economy, the nature of the market, the number of competitors, the aggressiveness of the competitors, consumer influences, and advertising may affect the price ceiling. Generally, there are two approaches to determining a price ceiling—hit or miss and market research.

The hit-or-miss approach requires an estimate of a selling price based on the simple principle that it is often easier to lower prices than it is to raise prices. Therefore, for a new product, it may be better to put the product on the market with a little higher margin than the firm would normally sustain. If the market accepts the product at that price, the extra margin can be considered windfall or the price could be lowered to stimulate further market acceptance and buying. In the event that the market rejects the product at that price, it is simpler to remove the excess margin and lower the price. In this manner, risk has been lessened. One danger in reducing the price of a new product is giving the consumer the signal that the product may be a "failure" in the market. However, this risk is often less than the risk of turning the consumer off by raising the initial price for the product. When the firm raises the initial price, it gives a signal to the customer that, in effect, a form of bait-and-switch has gone on. In other words, the consumer will feel that the lower price was a come-on, and now that an inroad has been established in the market, the price is raised. This may turn off the consumer, especially if price was the motivating factor to buy to begin with.

The market research approach offers the benefit of minimizing the risk associated with the introductory price of a new product. However, it does not avoid the cost of doing the necessary research to determine the appropriate price. One point to be considered in establishing the price is to ask the question: What did the consumer do before this product was available? In this manner, the marketing department is trying to make a "value of benefits" determination to establish the appropriate price for the product. It steers the mind away from a strictly cost-based approach.

What if the Market Balks?

If the market will not accept the product at the established market price (that covers the cost and a desired margin), four alternatives are generally available:

1. Discontinue the product.
2. Accept a lower margin.
3. Reduce costs.
4. Differentiate the product from that of the competitors in the minds of the buyers.

The first two solutions generally should be used as fall-back positions. Reducing costs is always an acceptable alternative and should be reviewed continuously regardless of the market's reaction to the price. However, reducing costs may often be difficult, especially at the introduction date of a new product. Simply put, learning takes time, and achieving cost reduction often comes later in the process. The fourth alternative, product differentiation, though sometimes overlooked, is often the best.

Product Differentiation

Frequently, a product can be distinguished from competing products not on the basis of price but of other factors that may influence buying habits. Such factors may include:

- *Superior quality, or an emphasis on extra features or reliability.* Rolls-Royce has often been used as the prime example.
- *Better service.* At one time, Caterpillar built a tremendous market presence by stressing the fact that its equipment could be serviced within 24 hours at any location in the world.

- *Product performance.* A good example is the claim by BMW that it is the "ultimate driving machine."
- *Delivery time.* Federal Express's overnight delivery created a market niche.
- *Financing arrangements.* This method is frequently used with great success by the automotive industry. Low annual percentage rate financing has put a number of people into showrooms who might not otherwise have gone at that time.
- *Engineering and design help.* Many construction firms offer "prebid" assistance.
- *Packaging.* A professor at a major university wanted to sell a used Corvette, so he offered a package of two tickets to the premier football game and a car to get to the game in for several thousand dollars.

Product differentiation will work best under conditions in which price sensitivity is low. Several factors influence buyer sensitivity to price and are therefore considerations in product differentiation:

- The availability of comparable substitutes.
- The frequency of the purchase of your product by an individual buyer.
- The impact of the purchase on the buyer's budget.

If competing products are not readily available, sensitivity to price diminishes. Price sensitivity increases as the frequency of purchase increases. And, if the product does not have a significant impact on the individual's budget, it will be less price sensitive.

Pricing as Part of Strategic Planning

A pricing philosophy is not a separate document to be placed alongside a strategic plan or an operating plan. Pricing is a management tool in every sense. It is a means of attaining your objectives rather than an objective itself. A pricing strategy, therefore, should become an integral part of planning for your product, market, and profit. In order to establish a written strategy for pricing, you may consider the following:

Operating Environment

- Establish whether the industry in which you operate is stable or fluctuates. If it fluctuates, you should try to determine what drives the fluctuations.
- Establish what the trend is in the industry for growth and the introduction of new products into the market.
- Where do you stand in the industry? Is yours the oldest company? Is it the leader? Is it the smallest?
- How innovative are you and the industry with new products?

Marketing Strategy

- How is the industry structured? How many companies together command 80 percent of the market? How many smaller firms are there? Where do you intend to emphasize your products and position?
- Is brand loyalty a key factor in the business? Is it your intention to concentrate on the wholesale market or do you intend to deal directly with the retail customers?

Product Strategy

- What market do you intend to target your products for? How extensive a product line do you intend to manufacture or carry?

Profit Strategy

- What economic factors will affect your products? Is the market for raw materials unstable, or is it showing the pressures of an expanding industry by increasing prices?
- Can you substitute less expensive raw materials, such as plastics, for steel to lower the cost to produce?
- Are incremental profit opportunities available for a budget segment of your product line? Is the market in which you operate very stable for revenue profit projections?

Once these considerations have been made, the process of developing a pricing philosophy should begin with describing and defining the market price patterns and overall price environment (retail, wholesale, etc.). Next, take your own internal corporate, market, product, or other plans and consider each of them for potential pricing actions. This will be discussed later.

To improve internal strategies, for instance, you must give full recognition to how price works in the market and then decide how and when to follow these established practices and when to strike out on your own using new pricing ideas, which vary from tradition. Only then does pricing become a tool that is part of your strategies rather than a stand-alone plan.

Master Checklist of Key Factors That Affect Pricing

The foundation for analyzing key factors lies in these questions:

- What information do I need?
- Where do I look for it?
- How do I get it?
- Who will have the information?
- How reliable is the source?

Once you have answers to these questions, you can proceed to analyze and use the information to make pricing decisions and devise strategies accordingly.

Internal Factors

Internal data and feedback are usually the most reliable pricing information. In order to accumulate sufficient data internally, feedback of information should be encouraged at all levels of management.

Customers and Users. Customers and users can be a good source of pricing information if the appropriate questions are asked and data are gathered. Ask such questions as:

- What do customers feel about the worth of the product?
- How much do they value the product? (It is important to remember that price is ultimately determined by the final consumer based on the concept of value received.)

- Understand how the buyers feel and what motivates them to buy. This calls for insight and perception. The most likely individual to possess that insight is the one who has to make that sale for a living.

Intermediate Customers.   If you sell to wholesalers, do not lose sight of the fact that resellers are really customers. These "middlemen" exert a profound influence on pricing decisions. You should continuously assess the following:

- What is going on with the business of the broker, agent, distributor, or dealer?
- Where are actual prevailing prices compared with list or suggested retail prices? An important matter to consider here is why there is a deviation between the manufacturer's suggested retail price and the prevailing market price.
- What unique pricing structures are prevalent? Are they becoming more complex? Areas to explore are the nature and basis for discounts, advertising, and promotional allowances; special terms; rebates; and occasionally indirect concessions relating to inventories, receivables, and payables.
- Are there any needed changes in the distribution channels?
- Are the middlemen doing the job for which they are being compensated, and are they bringing added value to the end user?

It is indeed important to work toward building a loyal, competent reseller network that keeps management supplied with necessary and well-founded information about the salability of products and the adequacy of pricing arrangements.

Company Developments.   Some of the keys to company developments include:

- New and replacement products.
- Shifts in objectives and financial targets.
- Regular sales reports and average actual selling price reports for the entire selling pipeline.

External Factors

Competition. Perhaps the most important information you need concerns the activities and pricing policies of competitors. No one should be more sensitive to the efforts of competitors than the sales force and regional sales managers. Focus on the following:

- *Pricing.* What are competitive price ranges for equivalent products, and how are the prices constructed in terms of discounts, allowances, and the like? Analysis should be made between prevailing and list prices for competitive products.
- *Innovation.* Are new products entering the market from competitors? In addition, are new uses being made of the existing products? Will minor modifications to your products better meet the needs of the current market? What changes are there in packaging, product features, delivery schedules, servicing, warranties, and a host of other areas?
- *Programs.* Are your competitors offering new sales promotion devices or sales force incentives to motivate sales of their products?
- *Markets.* Are competitors shifting into new markets or market segments and expanding their existing sales? What are the competitors' market share philosophies?
- *New competition.* Are there any new firms entering your industry or your market?

Overall Economic Trend. Market trends are the primary data needed to signal whether customers are willing and able to buy your products. Comparisons of historic trends between the overall market indicators and your sales will give some correlation between these two factors. With the use of this correlation, marketing can evaluate ongoing economic trends to project sales forecasts for the future. Price effectiveness is a direct result of gathering and analyzing meaningful data on future economic trends.

Trends in Substitute Products. Home buying and apartment rentals, at least in the short run, offer an example of trends in substitute products. It is important to look to the trend that may necessitate price shifts in order to maintain market shares. Remember, however, that these price shifts may be only temporary substitutes for the necessary innovation needed to maintain current market.

Effective Strategies to Combat Profit Erosion

Often, negative market reaction to a price increase can be offset by stressing the addition of more value to the product. Frequently, a business will advertise that its product is "new and improved" to give the impression that additional quality has been added to justify the price increase. This approach emphasizes the concept that the price is more reflective of the market value than of the cost. With this approach, you attempt to show that you are reacting to the market's need for a higher-quality product and, consequently, the price is reflective of that additional value.

Profits may erode due to market reaction to prices or price changes.

1. You may wish to announce new prices, but delay their effective date for 30 days. Any orders placed in that 30-day period will be honored at the current, lower prices. This strategy, commonly referred to as *grandfathering*, serves the useful purpose of accelerating sales for the next month from price-conscious customers. Therefore, even at a lower price, you will be receiving the benefit of accelerated cash flows. If price increase is based on anticipated increases in cost, there will be little erosion in profits in the short term because a decrease in buying at a higher price will be offset by the older, lower embedded cost.

2. Another strategy often used to offset the effects of an increased price is to unbundle services or options. You do not raise the price for the existing base product or service. However, the services or options that once were included as part of the price are now spun off as differentially priced items. Thus, the seller is offering the service or option at an additional cost.

   As an example, assume you have traditionally sold a product with a one-year warranty included. You may "unbundle" nine months of the warranty and offer the product with a three-month warranty at the old price and an extended nine-month warranty at an additional cost.

3. Another strategy is to maintain the price but to decrease the quantity in the package. For example, a 15-ounce package of Soapies has sold for $1.50, or $.10 per ounce. If the price per box ($1.50) is maintained but the box content is reduced to 12 ounces, the price per ounce has increased by 25 percent to $.125 per ounce.

4. A combination strategy is to increase prices per unit slightly and to decrease unit content simultaneously. This appears to have been the approach of candy bar manufacturers several years ago.

5. On some large-ticket items, consumers are more concerned with the payment amount than with total price. Therefore, making financing arrangements for extended terms, which hold payments, rather than price, at a constant level, may mask a price increase.

6. An interesting strategy can be effected when the product is sold primarily through vending machines. Because of the operation of the machine, prices can go up only in preset increments. For example, the minimum increase to the price of a bag of chips now priced at $0.50 is $.05, or 10 percent.

Municipalities have employed a variation of this strategy with parking meters. In addition to raising the price per minute, some meters accept only certain coins. Therefore, the consumer cannot buy just the quantity desired, and the effective price per unit to the consumer is increased by time left on the meter.

Summary

The cost of producing a product has a great deal to do with pricing, for if a company cannot price above cost, it cannot stay in business. Factors outside the business influence the price at which the company may sell its products or services. The price floor—that price below which one cannot sell and still make a profit—can be set using several pricing formulas set out in this chapter. Other pricing methods have been developed to attempt a target rate of return on investment or a target margin.

A company can more easily attain its targeted margins on products sold if it uses a target costing system to ensure that product costs meet expectations. This reduces the risk of missing profitability goals due to an excessive cost of goods sold. However, this concept must be applied not only to the new product design process, but also continually thereafter, since product costs will gradually stray from their budgeted levels, which will require periodic corrective action.

The other half of the pricing problem is the price ceiling—the price set by the market above which the product generally will not sell. Many factors affect price ceilings and usually a marketing research approach can estimate this market or ceiling price.

Techniques have been developed to minimize the adverse effect of consumer rejection of price increases. One can discontinue the product, accept a lower margin, reduce costs, or attempt to differentiate the product. Discontinuing a product is rather radical (but sometimes necessary); accepting a lower margin may not compensate for the risk and an effort toward lower costs should always be encouraged. The emphasis on product differentiation can exploit whole submarkets for existing products or product lines. Sometimes carving out a previously indistinguishable part of a bigger market may give a company a product advantage that may comfortably justify higher prices. One clear example is emphasis on product quality—priced a bit more but well worth it.

Pricing an integral part of market strategy, should occupy a position in a company's strategic plan. One must consider the effects of many external factors, such as competition, the overall economy, and trends in the introduction of and change in competitive and substitute products.

One should constantly monitor the market's reaction to the product and the price. Where profits start to erode, a change in strategy can combat this erosion and neutralize the consumer's resentment or reaction to a change in price. Explore such methods as packaging changes, like the reduction in coffee cans from 16 ounces to 13 ounces, to unbundling "extras" and grandfathering existing prices for a certain time before new prices become effective. The emphasis, again, is on planning for change—not crisis management.

Chapter 5

Managing Inventories

Introduction

The proper management and use of inventory is one of the most important functions in a company. When managed correctly, an inventory system keeps the overall inventory investment to a minimum, while maintaining a sufficient quantity of stock to meet the demands of customers. It is difficult to meet both of these goals, because they are in conflict with each other. A small investment in inventory means that only a small quantity of parts and products can be kept on hand, whereas good customer service appears to mandate large on-hand balances of anything customers may want, so that there are never any inventory stock-outs that could inconvenience a customer.

In this chapter, we will explore how to balance both goals, which we accomplish by maintaining a very high level of inventory accuracy, combined with the use of one or more manufacturing planning systems that force a company to purchase only what it needs for immediate production requirements. We also cover several related topics, such as safety stock levels, economic order quantities, and the role of bills of material and production schedules in the maintenance of proper inventory levels.

Perpetual Inventory

The most basic step that a company must first complete before it can delve into more advanced methods of inventory reduction and customer service is to attain a very high level of inventory accuracy. This is defined as inventory that is stored in the correct locations, is properly identified, and has the correct quantities. If any of these three items is incorrect, then the inventory item to which it refers is judged to be inaccurate in total. Using these criteria, a company should target a *minimum* accuracy level of 95 percent.

The reason for having such a high degree of accuracy is that several other key departments rely on this information to perform their functions. The purchasing department needs to know what inventory is on hand, so that it will know how much more to purchase. If the in-house inventory figures are always incorrect, then the purchasing staff will feel justified in continually assuming that there is no inventory in stock and will therefore buy more than is really needed. This will increase a company's investment in inventory, which is the reverse of one of the two inventory-related goals noted in the introduction. Also, the production department will run out of parts if the warehouse has fewer items on hand than is indicated by the inventory records, which will shut down production. When this happens, customers will not receive their orders on time, which goes against the other main inventory goal. Thus, one must work toward extremely high levels of inventory accuracy in order to form the foundation for a good inventory system.

The best way to create a completely accurate inventory is to reorganize it and then use cycle counting to ensure that the high level of accuracy reached through the reorganization is retained. The 12 reorganization steps are as follows:

1. *Install and test inventory tracking software.* The best way to maintain the accuracy of the inventory is to record all inventory-related information in a database that keeps track of inventory locations, quantities, and transaction histories. Consequently, the first step in the process is to develop a list of criteria for the functions a company needs in its inventory tracking system, review a group of

commonly used software packages to find the one that best fits these criteria, and test the best one to ensure that all promised functions actually exist. There is no need to custom-design an inventory database, since there are so many good packaged systems already available from software suppliers.

2. *Train the warehouse staff.* The people who will reorganize and update the accuracy of the inventory are the warehouse staff. Since they will be responsible for all systems surrounding the inventory, they must be completely informed of all steps that will be followed to reorganize and maintain the inventory, the timing and resources required for both the initial project and all ongoing maintenance activities, and their exact roles in the process. This requires detailed and ongoing meetings with all of these employees, starting at the beginning of the project and extending through it as new and refresher training becomes necessary. The ultimate success of the inventory accuracy effort depends on these people, so the importance of training and working with them cannot be overemphasized.

3. *Revise the warehouse rack layout.* Most warehouse racking systems grow in a disorderly manner, with a few racks being added as extra storage requirements come to light. This results in a haphazard warehouse layout that can be restrictive, a safety hazard, or just not the most economical use of space. To correct this, the racks should be laid out with sufficient space between them for forklift access (if such access is required), as well as the elimination of spots where inventory is stacked several levels deep, so that no one can tell what is located in the levels furthest to the rear. It may also be possible to add shelves to the existing racks, so that empty space is better utilized, as well as replace poorly constructed racks with ones that can sustain the storage of heavier loads.

4. *Create rack location codes.* Once the racks are in place, each bin must be identified with a location code. The most common coding system is to identify the left and right sides of an aisle with a letter. For example, the first aisle is "A," the second aisle is "B," and so on. Next, assign a number to each rack in the aisle, with all the even numbers on one side and the odd numbers on the other. For example, the first rack on the left side of aisle "A" will be designated

"A-01" and the first rack on the right side of the aisle will be coded "A-02." By using this approach, someone who is picking items in location sequence can reach to the left or right to find items at the front of an aisle, rather than walking all the way down one side and then back down the other. Finally, use another letter designation to identify the various levels of each rack. For example, if there are four levels in the racking system, then the bottom one will be coded "A," the next one "B," the next one "C," and the highest one "D." Thus, the second rack level in the first rack on the right side of the "A" aisle will be coded "A-02-B." This coding system designates a unique location code for every location in the warehouse. Since this can be a difficult layout to understand, we have included a sample warehouse chart in Figure 5.1 that lists the aisle and rack configurations for a typical warehouse. Also, to better illustrate the use of coding specific bin locations within an aisle, we have included in Figure 5.2 a side view of the left side of the aisle A that was previously noted in Figure 5.1.

5. *Create warehouse security.* Install a fence around the inventory storage area, as well as a gate that is shut and locked at all times. By doing so, people from outside the warehouse cannot remove inventory. This is a major issue, because all removals from inventory must be logged out of the inventory database. If this is not done, the accuracy of the database will rapidly drop. At the same time the fence is installed, the warehouse manager should also consider, creating an inventory issue desk, so that production or materials handling personnel can request inventory from a warehouse staff person who is stationed there, and who will log out all inventory issued by this means.

6. *Consolidate parts.* Review the entire warehouse area to see if the same parts are being stored in multiple locations. If so, consolidate them into a single location. By doing so, it is much easier to find, package, and count parts, which make the next few steps much easier to complete.

7. *Assign part numbers to products.* Once the parts have been consolidated, it is much easier to complete the next step, which is identifying each item and labeling it with the correct part number. This is usually a difficult and lengthy process, for some parts may be so

FIGURE 5.1

Top-Down View of Rack Location Codes

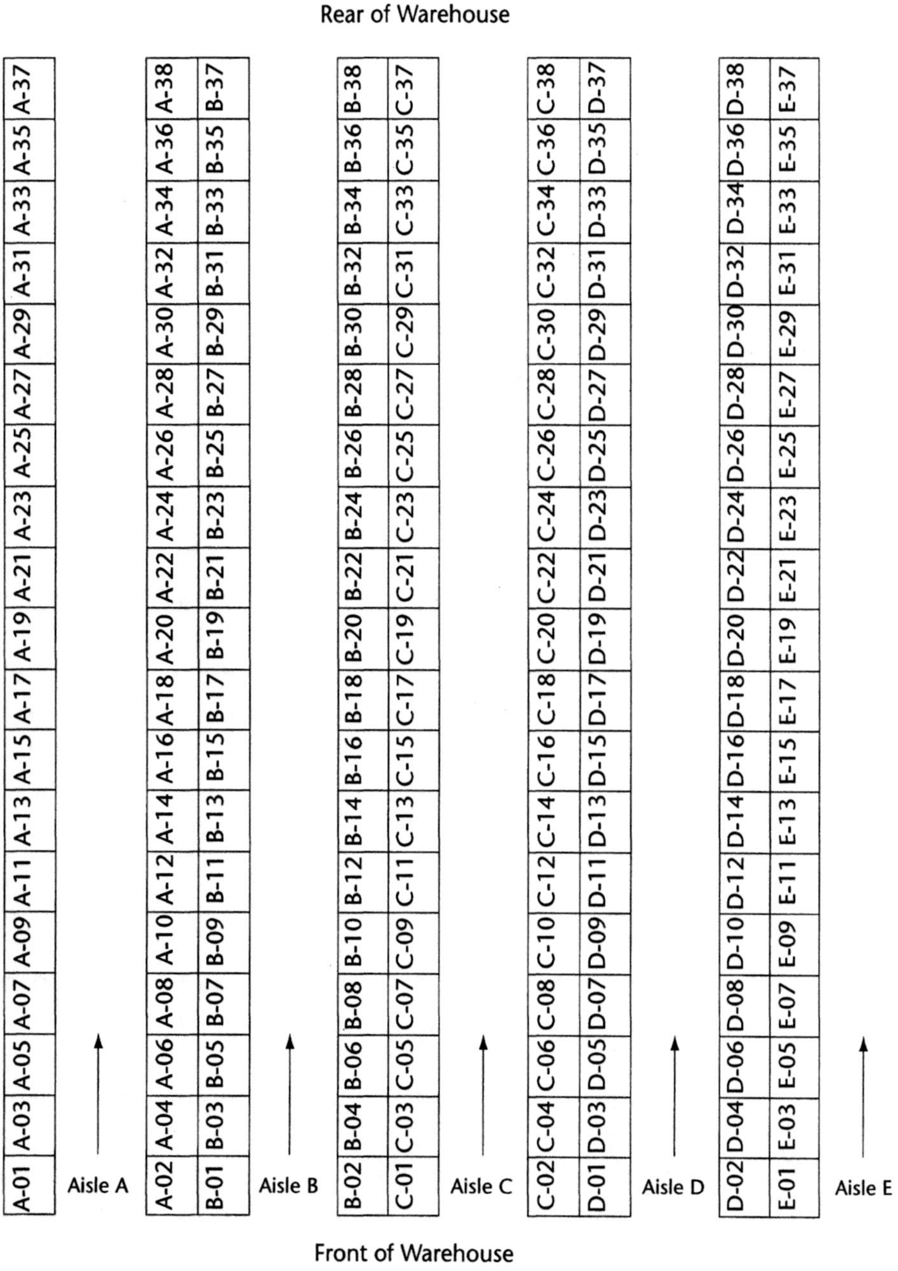

Rear of Warehouse

| A-37 A-35 A-33 A-31 A-29 A-27 A-25 A-23 A-21 A-19 A-17 A-15 A-13 A-11 A-09 A-07 A-05 A-03 A-01 |
↑ Aisle A |
| A-38 A-36 A-34 A-32 A-30 A-28 A-26 A-24 A-22 A-20 A-18 A-16 A-14 A-12 A-10 A-08 A-06 A-04 A-02 |
| B-37 B-35 B-33 B-31 B-29 B-27 B-25 B-23 B-21 B-19 B-17 B-15 B-13 B-11 B-09 B-07 B-05 B-03 B-01 |
↑ Aisle B |
| B-38 B-36 B-34 B-32 B-30 B-28 B-26 B-24 B-22 B-20 B-18 B-16 B-14 B-12 B-10 B-08 B-06 B-04 B-02 |
| C-37 C-35 C-33 C-31 C-29 C-27 C-25 C-23 C-21 C-19 C-17 C-15 C-13 C-11 C-09 C-07 C-05 C-03 C-01 |
↑ Aisle C |
| C-38 C-36 C-34 C-32 C-30 C-28 C-26 C-24 C-22 C-20 C-18 C-16 C-14 C-12 C-10 C-08 C-06 C-04 C-02 |
| D-37 D-35 D-33 D-31 D-29 D-27 D-25 D-23 D-21 D-19 D-17 D-15 D-13 D-11 D-09 D-07 D-05 D-03 D-01 |
↑ Aisle D |
| D-38 D-36 D-34 D-32 D-30 D-28 D-26 D-24 D-22 D-20 D-18 D-16 D-14 D-12 D-10 D-08 D-06 D-04 D-02 |
| E-37 E-35 E-33 E-31 E-29 E-27 E-25 E-23 E-21 E-19 E-17 E-15 E-13 E-11 E-09 E-07 E-05 E-03 E-01 |
↑ Aisle E |

Front of Warehouse

113

FIGURE 5.2

Side View of Rack Location Codes

Side View of Aisle A

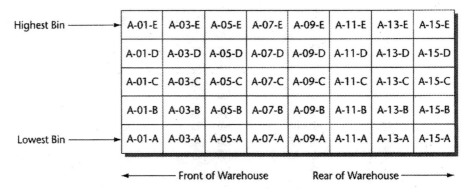

old that they are unidentifiable, while others may have previously been mislabeled. Also, during the labeling process, more parts will be identified that are the same thing, but are stored separately, and so there will be some additional consolidation of parts, not to mention the disposal of some items that are clearly so old or obsolete that there is no point in including them in the new inventory database.

8. *Package the parts.* Now that all parts have been identified, we are still not yet in a position to count them. First, we must package as many of the parts as possible in order to ease the counting task. For example, a bin full of screws can be separated into clusters of a thousand each (using a weigh scale) and bagged separately. Each bag is then stapled shut and marked with the quantity of its contents. Also, the contents of all boxes should be counted; then they should be sealed with tape and the quantity marked on the tape. By using this approach, the counting teams will have a much easier time counting parts. Also, cycle counters will later be able to use the packaged parts to ease their counting chores. Any counter will also know that any bag or box that has been opened must henceforth be completely counted to ensure count accuracy.

9. *Count all parts.* Now that the parts have been completely organized and identified, the task of counting the inventory is much easier. We will separate this task into a count of each item and the next task, which is writing down the count. In this step, have the warehouse staff walk through the racks and affix a label to each cluster of parts, noting the total number of units in each cluster. If anyone removes or adds parts to a cluster between this step and the next, then they must mark the change on the label. This step should be *immediately* followed by the next step.

10. *Compile the inventory data.* Create a standard set of prenumbered data entry sheets that list the part number, description, unit of measure, and quantity for each item in stock. Then schedule a time when there is no warehouse activity, such as a weekend, and use these sheets to record the entire inventory at that time. It is best to use counting teams of two people each, so that one person counts and one person writes, which tends to result in more accurate data. One counting team should be assigned to each aisle, and turn in their prenumbered sheets as soon as they have completed an assigned aisle. These sheets are then reviewed to see if anything is missing and are then turned over to the data entry staff for entry into the computer system.

11. *Enter all data in the software.* With a complete list of all inventory data in hand, it must now be entered in the inventory tracking software as quickly as possible. If the amount of collected information is large, then this will probably require the services of several data entry clerks, who may also require advance training in how to use the software. This step must be completed quickly, for the resulting inventory database must be used by the warehouse staff as soon as the next production shift commences.

12. *Review the data.* The data entry step probably involved the entry of thousands or tens of thousands of parts and their quantities in the inventory database. If so, it is very likely that some of those entries were incorrect. It is a major chore to locate and correct every error, but there are a few simple steps that can locate the most blatant errors. To do so, print out a list of the entire inventory database, including all entered information. Skim through all of the quantity fields and circle any inordinately large quantities for further

review. Also skim the unit of measure field for unusual or out-of-place units of measure (such as an "each" in the middle of a cluster of "yard" units of measure) and circle them for further review. Finally, if it is possible to sort the list by declining dollar order, review the most expensive items to see which ones are inordinately high, and circle them, too. Check the underlying detail for all circled items and correct entries as needed. All other errors will be caught and corrected during the periodic cycle counts, which we will commence after the initial setup of the inventory database.

Once these 12 steps have been completed, a company will have an accurate inventory database. However, the accuracy level will begin to drop rapidly unless the warehouse manager also institutes an ongoing cycle counting policy. Cycle counting is one of the most important tasks that the warehouse staff can undertake. It involves the continual counting of a small number of inventory items each day, with any counting variances being throughly investigated and corrected. The usual procedure is to print out a complete inventory list at the beginning of each day that is sorted by inventory location. The cycle counter is counting in order of inventory locations, and so will highlight all inventory on the list that islocated in the next few bins after those that were counted the previous day. The counter compares the actual inventory locations, part numbers, and quantities in the selected bins to those listed on the printout, with any differences being recorded as errors. The counter then computes the accuracy percentage and posts this on a chart in the warehouse area, so that everyone can see it. It is advisable to reward the warehouse staff if the accuracy level beats predetermined target levels, though the internal audit or accounting staffs should verify the results to ensure that the accuracy percentages are accurate—otherwise, the inventory counters will be rewarding themselves! The final and most important step in the cycle counting process is to determine *why* there were differences between the actual and database results. This is a very difficult process that may not always result in an answer. The cycle counter must review all inventory transactions in the computer for any problem part, interview other warehouse staff, and perhaps use educated guesses to determine the cause of a problem. Then the warehouse manager must use this information to correct the underlying problem, so that it does not occur again. This iterative process is the only way to attain a highly accurate inventory database that all parts of the company can use in the conduct of its business.

Before we continue with a discussion of ways to reduce the inventory investment while increasing customer service, we will address in the next four sections a series of small topics that relate to the management of inventory. All of these areas must be addressed when improving the accuracy of the inventory database, since they contribute to either the number of items counted, the manner in which inventory counts are conducted, or the system for recording transactions.

Physical Inventory Count

From time to time, it will be necessary to conduct a physical inventory count, rather than the cycle counting procedure outlined at the end of the last section. This may be required by the outside auditors as part of their year-end audit, or in response to a request from senior management to reverse a series of poor inventory accuracy measurements. Whatever the reason, many companies must still conduct a physical inventory, either in part or encompassing the entire company, each year. In this section, we note the 12 main steps to follow in conducting a physical inventory. They are as follows:

1. *Assign responsibility.* There must be one person in charge of the entire physical inventory count. Otherwise, with so many people involved, possibly in multiple locations, it is difficult to coordinate count activities to ensure an accurate count. This person should be in a position that is closely tied to the handling or storage of inventory, such as the logistics or warehouse manager, and should be advised on counting procedures by the controller.
2. *Select count and clerical teams.* All of the members of every counting team should be from a position that deals with inventory every day and should not include any staff from any other parts of the company. This is because untrained personnel do not know what

they are counting and will probably misidentify and miscount some parts, possibly resulting in a lower level of accuracy than was the case before the count. The clerical staff who are involved in entering the resulting count information into the computer should be experienced data entry clerks with low keypunching error rates.

3. *Schedule count locations and dates.* It is generally best to conduct all physical counts for all targeted locations at the same time, because this frequently must coincide with a shutdown of the manufacturing facility, such as occurs during an evening or on a weekend or holiday. Also, if the physical count happens to be for the year-end audited financial statements, all counts *must* be held at the same time. These times and places should be scheduled as far in advance as possible, so that facilities can prepare for shutdowns and the assigned counting and clerical staffs can arrange for extra time at the company.

4. *Inform staff and suppliers of cutoffs.* One of the most critical steps in the physical count process is ensuring that there is a correct cut-off. This means that inventory that has just been received, but has not been logged into the warehouse, is not included in the inventory count, since it will be added again as soon as the count is completed, as part of the normal receiving procedure. Similarly, any shipments that are still located on the shipping dock, and for which no shipment transactions have been processed, must be included in the count, since they will later be removed from the inventory as part of the normal shipping procedure. If this step fails, it is very likely that there will be incorrect counts of all newly received or shipped inventory items, which will take a great deal of time to remedy. The best approaches to this step are to thoroughly instruct the receiving and shipping staffs in cutoff procedures, as well as to clearly mark all items not to be counted and to directly supervise the marking of these items.

5. *Segregate count areas.* Part of the cutoff task is to physically segregate all inventory areas that are to be counted and not counted, with signs prominently identifying each type of area. Most of the items not to be counted will be recently received items in the receiving area. Because there may be items throughout the company that

must be counted, the counting teams may need to review the entire facility the day before the count, in order to identify all inventory in advance, and mark it down on a map of the facility.

6. *Meet with count teams.* On the day of the physical count, meet with the members of all count teams to review the step-by-step procedures to be followed for the day, as well as the specific responsibilities of each count team. A clear communication of this information is the best possible way to avoid confusion between the various counting and clerical staff during the count.

7. *Commence counts.* The count supervisor uses a map of the warehouse, similar to the one shown earlier in Figure 5.1, to assign counting areas to specific count teams. A clerk issues to them a sequentially numbered set of counting tags, on which they record the part number they are counting, the quantity, unit of measure, and the initials of the person recording the count. They tape a copy of each tag to the item they have just counted, and retain the other copy. When they have completed a section, they return to the clerk, who takes receipt of their copies of all tags, checks off the areas on the warehouse map that they have counted, and then assigns them a new count area and a new set of tags. This process continues until all areas of the warehouse have been counted.

8. *Verify tags.* Once the count has been completed, the clerk verifies that all prenumbered tags have been accounted for. If any are missing, the responsible count teams are sent into the warehouse area to find them.

9. *Enter tags in database.* Another group of clerks then enters the contents of the tags into the computer system. Once this task is complete, they print out a summarized report that lists the total counted quantities for each item and compares them to the quantities that were already stored in the database, as well as the quantity variance between the two.

10. *Investigate resulting variances.* The count teams then use this variance report to recount any item for which there is a large variance between the physical count and the computer database. This may require a count by a different count team than the one that originally made each count, since the first team may have made a counting error that it will make again if asked to perform a second

count. The results of these second counts are entered into the computer database as the new and corrected physical count quantities.

11. *Process approved count quantities in database.* Up to this point, there are two sets of inventory figures in the computer system—the old computer records and the new physical count records. If the count supervisor is satisfied with the results of the physical count, then he or she authorizes the substitution in the database of the old computer records by the new count records. This step will alter the on-hand quantities shown in the computer to match those just counted.

12. *Retain records.* In case later counting errors come to light, it is reasonable to retain copies of the count tags, as well as all reports showing count variances (there may be several successive versions), and the final physical inventory report that is run after all counts are completed.

It is very important to complete all of the steps listed here for a physical inventory, because missing one or more of them can result in an inventory that is less accurate after the count than it was before. In particular, any problem with the cutoff procedures can easily result in newly received inventory being accidentally double-counted or not counted at all. Also, there must be particularly tight control over the number of inventory count tags used, since missing any on which inventory quantities were recorded will result in an inventory database that has too few inventory items. Finally, and most important, only highly experienced warehouse personnel should be allowed to do a physical inventory count. This is because other employees do not have the same degree of familiarity with the inventory items and are likely to either record them with the wrong part numbers, assume incorrect units of measure, or miscount them. Using nonwarehouse personnel can result in pervasive errors in the results of the physical inventory.

The preceding steps can safely bring a company through a physical inventory count and should result in an improvement in the accuracy of the inventory database. However, it is much easier and more effective to use continuing cycle counts, as noted in the preceding section, because this approach does not conclude with a count—it targets and corrects underlying problems, which results in a degree of long-term inventory accuracy that a few physical inventory counts per year cannot hope to match.

Reducing the Inventory

The steps noted in the preceding two sections that relate to inventory counting practices may give one the impression that maintaining the accuracy of an inventory requires a great deal of labor. This is a correct impression. The more inventory a company stuffs into its warehouses, the more personnel will be required to keep track of it. These extra people represent an added overhead cost that adds no value to a company's products or services. Consequently, any efforts that can reduce the inventory will inevitably lead to a reduction in the number of personnel employed to track it, which will reduce expenses.

There are several ways to reduce inventory. One of the best is to remove fittings and fasteners from the warehouse, as well as the inventory database, and move them to the shop floor. This approach has several advantages. One is that the cycle counting staff no longer has to spend a large proportion of its time counting large quantities of inexpensive parts and can instead focus on more expensive items that are stored in smaller quantities—in short, those items that can stop a production line if there are none in stock. Also, the production staff no longer has to go to the warehouse, fill out a requisition for a few nuts or bolts, and wait at the warehouse gate for a stock picker to locate the items, log them out of the inventory database, and bring them to the requesting person. Instead, anyone in the production area can walk to a nearby rack of fittings and fasteners, immediately find what they want, and use it right away. There is very little move or wait time when these materials are made readily available to the production staff. These benefits make it very worthwhile to shift some inventory items to the production floor.

Unfortunately, there are some problems with storing inventory in the production area. One is that inventory shrinkage may increase, due to production workers' taking more parts than needed and throwing away the excess or by outright theft. However, the cost of this shrinkage should be small and can be reduced by stocking only inexpensive parts on the shop floor. If necessary, some management monitoring may also be necessary to spot repeat offenders. Another issue is that the inventory database can no longer be used to determine when the company is running short of certain parts, because the items are no longer recorded in the database. The best way to work around this problem is to store all parts on the shop floor in bins, each of which has a line painted inside it that indicates the point at which the part should be reordered. If the pile of parts within a bin has dropped to the point where the painted line is visible, then it is time to purchase more parts. A purchasing person can walk the production floor once a day, review the levels in all the bins, mark down those requiring refills, and then place orders with suppliers for refills. Another approach is to contract with a supplier to visit the company at regular intervals, refill the bins itself, and then bill the company for what it has already delivered. This approach avoids the need for a purchasing person and eliminates the turnaround time required to place an order and then wait for a delivery. A final problem is that the controller may object to taking items out of inventory, where they are recorded as assets, and expensing them to shop supplies, which results in an immediate one-time increase in the cost of goods sold. Though this expense will occur, it is a one-time expense and is generally small, since parts with a higher cost will be kept in the warehouse, where they will continue to be recorded as assets. All these issues are too small to pose a serious barrier to the shifting of selected inventory from the warehouse to the shop floor.

Another way to reduce the inventory is to compile several inventory usage reports from the computer system that reveal which items are not being used, and then sell some or all of these items back to suppliers. One report that accomplishes this is the "where used" report, which compares the on-hand inventory part numbers to the list of parts on all bills of material in the computer (see the Bill of Materials section later in this chapter), and returns a list of all parts that are not needed in any currently manufactured products. By default, the parts on this list should be eliminated. Some computer systems also contain a report that lists the last date on which a part was used, which provides some indication of the need for on-hand quantities. Yet another report lists the number of months' supply on hand, based on historical usage patterns. If none of these reports are available, it is always possible to physically review the inventory, looking for such items as old physical inventory tags, shipment dates, or other such identifying items on parts that are evidence of their age. No matter what method is used to find inventory that is no longer needed, the purchasing staff should then contact suppliers to see if they will take it back, usually for a credit against future purchases. A common fee for this service is a restocking charge of 15 percent. If suppliers will not take the inventory back, then the purchasing staff is faced with less palatable options, such as donating it for a tax deduction or declaring it obsolete and throwing it away. These are still better options than retaining the excess inventory, since it is expensive to store and insure it.

Both reducing the total amount of inventory through supplier restocking and shifting inventory to the shop floor are good approaches for shrinking the size of the inventory that must be regularly counted and updated. Two additional approaches are material requirements planning and just-in-time manufacturing, which will be covered in later sections of this chapter.

Picking and Backflushing

There are two ways to record the usage of inventory. Each method works best under very specific circumstances, and will have differing impacts on the timing of inventory transactions, error rates, and the accuracy of inventory records.

One way to record the usage of inventory is through the picking method. This is the most common approach used by businesses today. In essence, any movement of inventory out of the warehouse is assumed to be a transfer into the cost of goods sold, and the inventory is expensed off at that time. If any inventory is returned to the warehouse from the shop floor, then it is removed from the cost of goods sold and recorded in the inventory once again. This approach has the advantage of being nearly foolproof when set up and operated correctly. The warehouse staff knows that anything leaving the warehouse must be recorded in the computer system at once, as well as anything being returned. The warehouse staff is fully responsible for the accuracy of these transactions, since it moves everything in and out of the warehouse, and can be trained to record the moves whenever inventory passes through the gates of the warehouse. To make this system work, the computer system must be readily accessible to the warehouse staff, which means that there should be computer terminals located throughout the warehouse area for their use. There must also be a fence around the warehouse, with a locked gate and severely restricted access to the warehouse area, which forces tight control of inventory movements. Also, if the production staff is working nights or weekends, then there must be a trained warehouse person on site who will move inventory and record transactions. This approach has the advantage of great accuracy and the immediate recording of transactions, which keeps the inventory records up to date to within a few minutes of each transaction actually occurring. The downside of this approach is that a company must invest in an after-hours warehouse staff if the production department needs parts at all hours of the day. Also, transactions can be missed if the warehouse staff forgets to enter them in the computer; there may be an inordinate number of computer transactions if many small inventory moves are made out of the warehouse, and anyone wanting to obtain a part from the inventory must wait for the warehouse staff to get it for them, which involves some wait time. Despite these problems, this is a simple system that is easy to install, maintains good control over expensive inventory items, and works well in most facilities.

The alternative method is one that requires considerably more systems expertise and is called the backflushing method. Under this approach, the materials handling staff takes raw materials directly out of the warehouse and transports it to the production facility without entering any transactions in the computer system at all. Instead, the production scheduling staff calculates the quantity of products manufactured each day and enters this number into the computer, which uses product bills of material to automatically calculate the quantities of raw materials that must have been used, and deducts these amounts from the inventory records. This method has the advantages of requiring little data entry, allowing direct access to inventory without any waiting at the warehouse gate, and eliminating the need for any after-hours warehouse staffing, since they no longer make computer entries. However, there are several serious problems with this approach that should restrict its use to only the best-run production operations. One is that the number of units produced each day, on which the entire system is based, must be accurately counted and entered into the computer or else the inventory records will become severely inaccurate. Another issue is that the bills of material, on which the backflushing calculation is also based, must be completely accurate or else the same problem will arise. Further, scrap must be carefully tracked, either separately or through the bills of material; otherwise, this will also gradually throw off the inventory balances. In addition, there is a time delay in the processing of the backflushing transaction. Given the computer time required to perform backflushing, most companies run it only once a day, which means that the inventory records will be off by the amount of any withdrawals from stock during the current day. These are significant problems that can lead to severe inventory inaccuracies in short order, so a company must be certain of the excellence of all its inventory-related systems before implementing a backflushing system.

Of the two inventory transaction recording systems presented here, the easiest one to install and maintain is the picking system. The backflushing system, though the inherently more elegant system (due to the minuscule amount of data entry needed), can easily reduce the accuracy of the inventory database if any related systems do not run properly, and therefore is recommended only for world-class manufacturing operations.

Obsolete Inventory

Obsolete inventory is a major problem in industries in which products and their components rapidly become dated by new and technologically more advanced products. This is a particular problem in the personal computer industry, where computer models are replaced as frequently as once a month. When this happens, all old stocks are immediately rendered obsolete, which means that their values drop precipitously, causing an increase in the cost of goods sold when they are written off. In this section, we explore ways to prevent inventory obsolescence from occurring, so that companies will not incur large and unexpected losses that are due to this problem.

To stop inventory obsolescence, we must first understand why it occurs. One major reason is that the engineering department alters the design of an existing product, so that an existing part is replaced by a new one. When this happens, no one checks to see if there are any existing quantities of the old part left in stock, so that any remaining inventory will never be used. This problem can be remedied by forcing the engineering staff to work with the purchasing department whenever it designs a product change, so that old parts are first cleared out of stock before new parts are used. Another reason for obsolescence is that the purchasing department is buying more parts than needed for current production requirements. It does this to avoid the cost and effort of placing many orders for smaller amounts, instead of placing just one or two orders for large quantities. The danger in placing these large orders is that new production runs may never arise, which leaves the excess part quantities in the warehouse with no other possible use. The best way to fix this problem is to require the purchasing staff to purchase only quantities sufficient to match current needs, which is greatly aided by a material requirements planning system (see the section later in this chapter). Yet another way in which obsolete inventory can arise is when customers place orders, against which the purchasing staff buys parts in anticipation of production, only to have the customers pull their orders; the purchase orders for parts are not cancelled by the company, so the parts arrive at the receiving dock, even though there is no longer a use for them. To resolve this problem, a company can either force its customers to honor their purchase orders, or use a material requirements planning system to automatically notify the purchasing staff when they have open purchase orders for parts that are no longer required by any open customer orders.

Obsolete inventory can also arise when there is an imbalance between the production quantities in different machines in the production process. When this happens, a few machines will produce more parts than are needed by downstream machines, which run at a slower rate. If the entire production line changes over to a new product without using up these excess parts, then they will be sent to the warehouse, where they will probably never be used, since it is too much trouble to remove them from storage and send them to the proper machines for finishing work when the manufacture of that product eventually starts up again. This problem also arises between the production facility and any downstream assembly operations, since the manufacturing operation as a whole may create more products than the assembly staff can finish, which may result in the same problems. In both cases, the solution is to use detailed production scheduling to balance the speed of production of all aspects of the production and assembly processes, so that excess part quantities do not accumulate anywhere.

The causes of obsolete inventory lie in many places—purchasing, engineering, and production scheduling. It takes excellent control over all three functions to keep obsolete inventory to a minimum, which requires good management, systems, and training to attain.

Safety Stock

Having reviewed a number of issues related to the maintenance of a highly accurate inventory database, we can now return to the issues of reducing the inventory investment while improving customer service. One of the most time-honored approaches to improving customer service through the use of inventory has been the concept of safety stock. Under this approach, a company retains an excess amount of stock on hand in order to ensure that no customer must ever wait for an order to be filled. In this section, we review the circumstances under which this approach works best and how it can be improved.

Safety stock is most effective in situations in which customers arrive with no notice and expect to have their orders filled at once. This is most common in a retailing environment, such as a hardware store, where customers expect to purchase screws, nails, electrical parts, or other similar items without being turned away due to a stock-out. In these businesses, having the right parts on hand at all times is critical. Or is it?

The use of safety stock is, to a large extent, driven by the expectations of the customer. For example, if a hardware store advertises itself as being a deep discounter, customers will go there in order to find bargain purchases. If an item is out of stock, then they may very well come back another day, because the anticipated savings on later purchases are so great that the extra trip is not considered an inconvenience. If the retailer were to be a deep discounter as well as attempt to provide better service by investing in safety stock, then the cost of the extra inventory would cut into its profits, possibly making the entire business plan untenable. However, a hardware store that prides itself on superior customer service will have a much better case for using safety stocks. Its customers (probably an entirely different group than those going to the deep discounter) will be willing to pay a premium on the expectation that they will find anything they want at the store every time they shop there. For this type of customer, it makes a great deal of sense to make the extra investment, because the higher margins warrant the cost of the inventory. Thus, the company strategy drives the use of safety stock, which can be an excellent tool for improving customer service but is nothing more than an added cost when used with the wrong strategy.

The problem with safety stock is its considerable cost. This cost is not just the money tied up in the extra inventory investment. In addition, the cycle counting team must count the extra part quantities, which is an added labor cost. Also, some of the parts will be damaged or destroyed, while some parts may never be used at all, which results in their being scrapped. Further, they require an extra investment in rack space, as well as a small amount of additional insurance to cover replacement costs. In most cases, the annual cost of inventory is roughly 25 percent of its initial purchase price, so it can be a very expensive item to keep on hand. Given the excessive cost of any kind of inventory, a good way to keep the cost of safety stock low is to summarize the per-unit cost of each inventory item for which there is a need to keep safety stock on hand, and sort this list in increasing dollar order. Usually, the bulk of the items on the list are so inexpensive that a company can keep large stocks on hand with little investment. For the small minority of items that comprise the bulk of the safety stock investment, management can maintain a much higher level of control. This control may involve many small replenishment orders, which avoids the need for a large safety stock, or else taking a risk on the occasional inventory stock-out in exchange for a smaller safety stock investment. The best safety stock level can be determined over time by gradually reducing the amount on hand until a stock-out occurs or by keeping detailed records regarding sales volumes by month, so that a quick review of sales for the last year will pinpoint the greatest sales level against which to be adequately stocked. By using this approach, a company can maintain an adequate level of safety stock on the vast majority of its items, while closely monitoring its inventory investment in a small number of its costliest products.

Thus far, we have assumed that safety stock is used only for items that are to be sold to customers. This does not involve safety stock for components that are included in finished goods. Creating safety stocks for such component parts is not a good idea, because they are wholly dependent on the demand for the products of which they are components; since this demand is completely predictable through the production schedule (see the Production Schedule section later in this chapter), there is no need to maintain additional safety stock for unpredictable demand. There are good manufacturing planning systems on the market (made by such software suppliers as SAP, Baan, Oracle, PeopleSoft, Fourth Shift, and J. D. Edwards): that will decompose a production schedule into a lower-level demand schedule for all component parts and even place purchase orders with suppliers for missing parts with sufficient lead times to ensure their delivery prior to the planned production date. Given this level of sophistication, there is little need for safety stock for parts that are included in company-built products.

Safety stock remains a valid concept for products that have uncertain demand levels, but it should be confined to those companies whose strategies are built on high levels of customer service, since this extra inventory can be expensive to maintain. It is not an appropriate concept for component parts, since demand for these items is predictable.

Economic Order Quantities

Prior to the advent of manufacturing planning systems, the best way to order parts was with an economic order quantity (EOQ). This is a formula that factors in the holding and ordering costs for an inventory item and determines the precise purchasing quantity at which the combined holding and ordering costs are at the lowest possible level. The formula for the EOQ is *the square root of:*

$$\frac{(2) \times \text{(Expected demand for the period)} \times \text{(Cost of placing order)}}{\text{(Cost of holding one unit in stock for the period)}}$$

For some products, the expected demand for the period may vary considerably by period. For example, the demand for hockey sticks will peak in the winter and melt away in the summer. For products such as these, the expected demand part of the EOQ formula may require frequent correction. For other products with less seasonality, an annual average will be sufficient.

Doing the Math for EOQ—A "Case Study"

To demonstrate the use of the foregoing information, let's build an example and see how the calculations might work in a "real life" situation. For this, we transport ourselves to a nearby campus and to the fraternity house of a group of scholars well known for their devotion to mathematical models and beer and commonly known as the DUI house. One of its members, having achieved the status of junior in the local business school, has recently been exposed to some concepts of inventory management. Ever watchful for topics suitable for term papers, this scholar has gathered the following information concerning some items of inventory moving through the rather large cooler attached to the kitchen of the house.

- The house purchases "industrial strength" beer shipped directly from the brewery in the Rocky Mountains to the house in 50 gallon drums. Delivery time is usually one week.
- Average purchases for the last three years have been 100 drums, or 5,000 gallons per year.
- The house usually orders 10 drums at a time, placing the order when they have 10 drums on hand.

- The price paid is $5.00 per gallon, including transportation from the Rocky Mountains. The cost of placing each order averages about $25.00. This cost includes the time spent each week checking the level in the barrels, notifying the chef, who sends a requisition to the fraternity president, letters and phone calls by the president to place the order, reassure himself that the order will be shipped, and expediting when necessary (due to his forgetfulness in placing orders on time), unloading the beer truck by the kitchen staff, testing for quality (usually accomplished by the same staff with the assistance of any members who happen to have seen the truck arrive), and the usual costs associated with writing checks and getting them approved by the faculty adviser, who must be reconvinced each time that the expenditure really is a necessity.
- Warehousing costs include $200 per month, the amount necessary to cover building and maintaining a 20,000 cubic-foot walk-in refrigerator, $100 per month for electricity to operate the refrigeration unit, and $100 per month for kitchen labor assigned to taking care of things that may be placed in the cooler.
- The house has received its insurance bill for the coming year and the company has noted the addition of the cooler and responded by raising their rate on the house by $50 per month plus 1 percent of the value of items kept in the cooler.
- At present the house seldom finds itself with more than 15 drums of beer on hand and the amount of storage space in the cooler used by these drums is approximately 750 cubic feet.
- The brewery has so far been able to hold the line on prices, but has informed the house that it should expect an annual price increase of approximately 3 percent for the foreseeable future.
- Although its account is negligible, the house is a member of the campus credit union and is eligible to receive interest at the rate of 7 percent on money deposited with the credit union.
- A member of the house majoring in physics is still running tests, but despite all theory offered to date, the chef assures the president that a shrinkage rate of $1/4$ of 1 percent of the inventory per month is entirely normal. Another member (a pre-med major) has offered the suggestion that blood tests on the chef might be more revealing than any test run to date.

• A spring snow storm once delayed the delivery truck causing the supply to be exhausted before new supplies arrived. This disaster resulted in a change of leadership in the fraternity and since that day 5 drums have been kept with locked spigots and chained to the wall as safety stock.

Now let's look over the shoulder of our scholar from the business school as he calculates EOQ for beer for the DUI house.

1. We know the equation for EOQ:EOQ $= \sqrt{(2 \times D \times O)/H}$ where D = demand, O is the cost of placing an order, and H is the cost of holding one unit in inventory for the period. The units that we have been using are gallons and the period we have been discussing is a year.
2. Records indicate that the amount used during the year is 5,000 gallons.
3. He has established the cost of placing an order at $25. This was done by adding the times necessary to perform all the functions associated with ordering from the initial recognition that supplies were low to the final accounting functions associated with paying for the order. A cost per hour (including overhead) was multiplied by the time taken for all these functions. To this were added other out-of-pocket costs for phone calls, mailing, and miscellaneous paper work.
4. Now he must calculate the costs of holding one gallon in stock for one year. This should be stated as a percentage of the value of one gallon. Several of our costs (such as cost of money, insurance, and shrinkage) are charged in terms of a percentage of value. However, others must be determined. Most important of these is the cost of storage space. This is done as follows:

Cost of the cooler:	$2,400 per year
Cost of utilities:	$1,200 per year
Cost of labor:	$1,200 per year
Cost of insurance:	$600 per year
TOTAL	$5,400 per year

As there are 20,000 cubic feet of space in the cooler, this works out to $.27 per cubic foot. As it takes approximately 1 $\frac{1}{2}$ cubic feet to store 1 gallon, storage costs per year, per gallon, are approximately $.40. This number is then divided by the cost per gallon of $5. The number thus obtained (.08) is the annual storage cost stated as a percentage of the cost per gallon.

5. We now add the other percentages for other costs such as insurance and shrinkage.

6. Now he must deal with inflation. Since the cost of beer is expected to rise, there may be some advantage to having it in inventory. He therefore subtracts the expected inflation from the other percentages. (Of course, if the price of beer had been expected to fall, the effect would have been detrimental, and the expected deflation rate would be added to the other costs). Now he adds up all the percentages:

Cost of money:	7%
Cost of warehouse:	8%
Cost of insurance:	1%
Cost of shrinkage:	3%
Cost of inflation:	3%(minus)
TOTAL	16%

7. The cost, then, of holding one gallon in inventory for one year (although we might hesitate to drink that particular gallon) is the percentage we have calculated multiplied by the cost of one gallon. This works out to be 16 percent of $5 or $.80.

8. Now he has the numbers to feed into the equation. Demand is 5,000 gallons, cost of placing an order is $25 and the cost of holding one gallon in inventory for one year is $.80. Therefore:

$$EOQ = \sqrt{\frac{(2 \times D \times O)}{H}} = \sqrt{\frac{(2 \times 5,000 \times 25)}{.8}} = 559$$

According to his calculations, the amount to order is 559 gallons per order.

Problems

But wait. All is not well. The house buys beer in 50-gallon drums and 559 gallons is not evenly divisible by 50. This leaves the choice of rounding up to 12 or down to 11 drums per order. While the choice could be made arbitrarily, it could also be made mathematically. The objective would be to calculate the sum of ordering costs and holding costs under each of these options and choose the one that is the least. We'll see how to do that later when we consider quantity discounts.

The second problem is that although the school operates four quarters in a year, the house is open only three of these quarters. The house closes for the summer quarter and is not used. Additionally, a rather extensive social season occasioned by rush parties and football parties in the fall results in approximately 3,000 gallons of the annual quantity being consumed in that quarter, the balance of the demand being spread rather evenly over the spring and winter quarters. This means that if the house orders based on an annual demand there will probably be excessive ordering costs in the fall quarter, excessive holding costs in the spring and winter quarters, and inventories left over in the summer.

Of course, if demand is then stated in terms of quarterly demand, holding costs must also be stated quarterly (or one-quarter of the annual holding costs). Now the calculations must be repeated.

For the fall quarter:

$$EOQ = \sqrt{\frac{(2 \times D \times O)}{H}} = \sqrt{\frac{(2 \times 3{,}000 \times 25)}{.2}} = 886 \text{ gallons}$$

For spring and winter quarters:

$$EOQ = \sqrt{\frac{(2 \times D \times O)}{H}} = \sqrt{\frac{(2 \times 1{,}000 \times 25)}{.2}} = 500 \text{ gallons}$$

We again see the necessity to round up or down. Notice that, as expected, when the demand was higher the orders were larger.

Adding Quantity Discounts to EOQ Calculations

Gathering the information and doing the calculations for economic order quantity under the conditions described above is a relatively simple process and has been used for over 50 years. The catch in the system is that most users do not know how to make it work under conditions where quantity discounts are offered. There is even a generation of very expensive software for tracking inventory and making purchasing decisions that cannot calculate for conditions of quantity discounts. If you have software that makes purchasing recommendations, a very easy test will determine whether or not it has this capability. If the software has no provisions for accepting information about quantity discounts, it stands to reason that such information cannot and is not being used in making the purchase recommendations. If this is the case, understanding and using a model that does take into account quantity discounts may result in considerable savings.

Unit Costs

Previously, it was not necessary to consider unit cost as part of the decision process because there was no change in unit cost with respect to order size. However, when quantity discounts are offered, the effect is to change the price per unit depending on the size of the order placed—with prices decreasing as order size grows. The graph shown in Figure 5.3 shows the effect of order size on unit cost (UC). For order sizes less than quantity A, the first price (UC_1) prevails.

For order sizes larger than A and smaller than B, the second, cheaper price (UC_2) prevails, and for orders larger than quantity B, the third (and cheapest) price (UC_3) prevails.

Holding Costs Revisited.   Because one of the components of holding costs was the cost of money used to buy the inventory, you should expect that as the cost of the units changes, the holding costs will change with it. The effect is shown in Figure 5.4. Notice that you began with an assumption of safety stock, but this time you have three lines—each of them depicting holding costs. Only the solid portion of each line should be considered because the unit costs that comprised

FIGURE 5.3

Effect of Order Size on Unit Costs

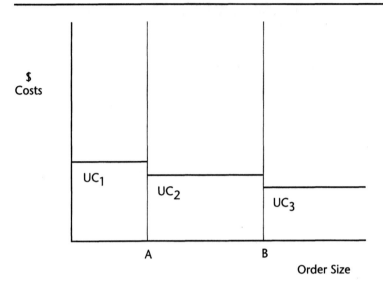

FIGURE 5.4

Effect of Order Size on Holding Costs

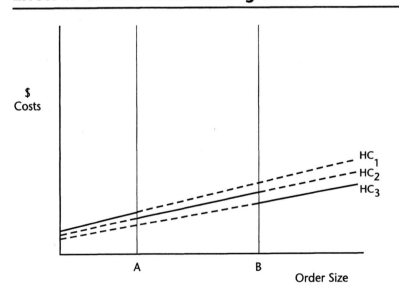

part of the calculation of holding cost is different for each quantity range.

Notice that the three lines do not have the same point of origin: although the same level of safety stock is applicable to all three, varying unit costs attach to that safety stock depending on the size of the order. Since the holding cost is in part related to the cost of the units, the same level of safety stock will have a variable holding cost depending on the price paid for the units in that safety stock. The three holding cost lines are referred to as HC_1, HC_2, and HC_3.

Ordering Costs Revisited. It is not necessary to construct a new graph for ordering costs because the costs of placing an order does not vary when the price of the unit ordered varies. This graph will remain the same.

Summation of the Graphs Revisited. If you graph the cost of the units, add to that the graph for order cost (unchanged), and add to that your new graph for holding costs, the graph summing these three really turns out to be three graphs (curves). This is shown in Figure 5.5.

FIGURE 5.5

Overall Effect of Order Size

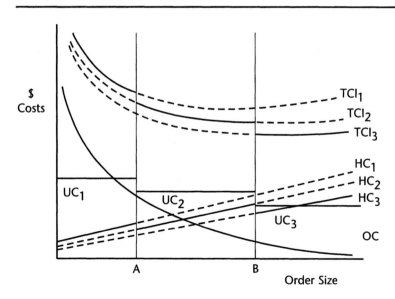

Figure 5.6

Simplified Overall Effect of Order Size

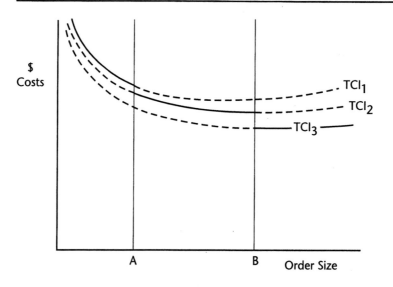

This is a rather messy looking graph and with all the dotted lines (which are irrelevant) is not very helpful. Let's remove the extra lines and look at only those relevant portions of the curves. This gives us Figure 5.6. Once again, the task is to find the point at which each curve reaches its minimum and then select the one that is the least of the three.

Notice that in the case depicted in this graph, the price breaks were sufficiently large, the ordering costs sufficiently high, and the holding costs sufficiently low so that the curve for TCI_3 is always the lowest and the purchaser is driven to buy at the lower price. This is not always the case. For example, it is possible for the lowest point of curve TCI_1, to be lower than some portions of either TCI_2 or TCI_3. Therefore, you should not assume from looking at the graph in Figure 5.6 that it will always be cheaper to buy at the high quantity/low price option.

This is where the calculations start to get a bit complicated. First calculate the lowest point (or indicated EOQ) for each of the curves. Next, make comparisons.

1. The lowest point on a curve may fall within the quantity range relevant to that curve. If this is the case, then that indicated EOQ is used for subsequent calculations.

2. The indicated EOQ may fall in the next higher range. If this is the case this quantity is considered "infeasible" and is not used. After all, if you are buying in that next-higher range, you would expect to pay a lower price and thereby be on the curve for that range.

3. The indicated EOQ may be in the range below the minimum quantity necessary to obtain the price used in the calculation. If this is the case, then the program needs to throw out the number calculated and use the lowest number that would get that price (the lowest number in that quantity range).

Completing the Calculations. Having calculated the indicated EOQs and made the above checks, you then test to see which of these numbers gives the lowest overall costs of inventory. For each case, calculate the total costs of the units purchased, add to that the total holding costs, and add to that the total ordering costs. These totals are compared and the order size resulting in the lowest total costs selected. This is the number finally referred to as "EOQ Under Conditions of Quantity Discounts."

Completing the Example

To see how these calculations work, let's return to the DUI house where the president is somewhat concerned over a letter he has recently received from the brewery. In the letter, the brewery states that it is changing its pricing structure. An examination of its records indicate a rather high cost in processing small orders, necessitating some changes in pricing. To begin with, it will no longer sell in quantities under 250 gallons.

The prices above 250 gallons are as follows:

LOWER LIMIT	UPPER LIMIT	PRICE PER GALLON
250	600	$6.00
650	1,000	$5.00
1050	none	$4.75

Now let's go through the calculations as described above.

(1) Calculate an EOQ for each of these prices. We will refer to these as EOQ_1, EOQ_2, EOQ_3 for these prices of $6.00, $5.00, and $4.75 respectively.

$$EOQ_1 = \sqrt{\frac{(2 \times 3{,}000 \times 25)}{(.04 \times 6.00)}} = \sqrt{\frac{150{,}000}{.24}} = 790$$

$$EOQ_2 = \sqrt{\frac{(2 \times 3{,}000 \times 25)}{(.04 \times 5.00)}} = \sqrt{\frac{150{,}000}{.20}} = 866$$

$$EOQ_3 = \sqrt{\frac{(2 \times 3{,}000 \times 25)}{(.04 \times 4.75)}} = \sqrt{\frac{150{,}000}{.19}} = 888$$

Having calculated the EOQ at each of these prices, notice that the only change in each of these equations was that of price. There was no change in the constant (2), the demand level, the ordering costs, or the holding cost percentage. The only change was in price.

Now put the calculated EOQs to the test previously indicated.

(A) The EOQ calculated for the $6.00 price was 790 units. However, as you check the pricing table you see that if you were to order at that level, you would be eligible for the $5.00 price, because the quantity indicated is above 650 gallons. It stands to reason that you would not order at this level and still expect to pay the $6.00 price. Therefore, discard this number and do not consider it anymore. In other words, you have now made a decision that whatever your order quantity, it will be more than 600 gallons. The 780 gallon purchase at $5.00 is considered "infeasible."

(B) The EOQ calculated using the $5.00 price was 866 units. This falls in the quantity range applicable to the $5.00 price and, therefore, you can consider the number. However, since you must order in multiples of 50 gallons, round this number to 850 for your further calculations.

(C) The EOQ calculated using the $4.75 price was 888 units. This is not a sufficient quantity to gain the $4.75 price. If you want that price, you must order a minimum of 1,050 gallons. Since you fell below that quantity, discard the 888 gallon calculation and use the lowest number which would gain the $4.75 price. That number is 1,050 gallons per order.

You now have two options remaining. You can either order 850 gallons per order at the $5.00 price or 1,050 gallons per order at the $4.75 price. To make this decision, calculate the cost of the beer, the cost of storage, and the cost of ordering for both options, sum these for each option, and choose the lesser of the two.

(2) In both cases you expect consumption to be 3,000 gallons. The cost of 3,000 gallons at $5.00 per gallon is $15,000 and the cost at $4.75 a gallon is $14,220.

(3) Now calculate holding cost. At $5.00 a gallon, your holding costs are 4 percent of $5.00 or $.20 per gallon per quarter. For the $4.75 price, the cost will be 4 percent of that price or $.19 per gallon per quarter. Now calculate the average inventory. Since this is equal to half the ordered quantity plus the safety stock, this will vary depending on the order size. For an order size of 850 gallons the average inventory will be half that, or 425 gallons + the 250 gallons held for safety stock, the total being 675 gallons. At an order level of 1,050 units, half that is added to 250 gallons for safety stock yielding a total of 775 gallons of average inventory. At the $5.00 price, then, multiply 675 gallons of average inventory by $.20 per gallon per quarter and you obtain a cost of $135 per quarter for storage. At the $4.75 price level, we multiply 775 gallons by $.19 per gallon, obtaining $147 per quarter storage costs.

(4) Now calculate ordering costs. You know that the cost of placing an order is $25.00. The number of orders placed is equal to the demand for the period divided by the amount ordered. For the lower order quantity, the number of orders placed is 3,000/850, which you multiply by $25.00 giving an ordering cost for the period of $88.00. At the higher order level, divide 3,000 by 1,050 and multiply that by $25.00, giving an ordering cost of $71.00. Notice that in both these cases the division yielded a whole number and a fraction. Since we are assuming that the DUI house is an ongoing operation, we can deal with fractional orders using the assumption that orders will also be placed in subsequent quarters. However, during spring quarter this

assumption is not valid because you don't want beer left during the summer. Therefore, the last order placed in the spring quarter will probably be for an amount in excess of 1,050 gallons.

(5) Now calculate the Total Cost of Inventory (TCI) for each of the two order quantities under consideration. Refer to these as TCI_2 and TCI_3.

$$TCI = \text{Unit Costs} + \text{Holding Costs} + \text{Ordering Costs}$$
$$TCI_1 = \text{Infeasible}$$
$$TCI_2 = 15{,}000 + 135 + 88 = \$15{,}233$$
$$TCI_3 = 14{,}220 + 147 + 71 = \$14{,}438$$

(6) Comparing the total costs of inventory under each of the two potential order quantities, you see that the house can save $785 during the fall quarter by choosing the 1,050 order quantity over the next most preferable quantity of 850 gallons. While these savings are considerable, we should not forget other considerations that may have an effect on the decision. If the house continues to keep 250 gallons of safety stock, the receipt of an order for 1,050 gallons will use almost all of the available cooler space, leaving little for other purposes. Of course, the savings of $785 realized during the fall quarter could be used to purchase a refrigerator. (This is an example of how some of the calculations used in inventory management can also be used to assist in justifications for capital purchases.) The house must also be aware that as the amount of inventory stored rises, the opportunity for undetected pilfering also rises. The house should probably consider purchasing additional locks for drums.

A significant failing of the EOQ model is that it assumes a continuing demand for an item, whereas it might actually be one that the engineering staff is phasing out or for which demand is rapidly dropping. In these cases, it is very important to keep the purchasing staff in close touch with the engineering and sales departments, respectively, so that information is exchanged regarding parts that will no longer be used. These special cases should override the quantities suggested by the EOQ formula, so that a company does not overpurchase and eventually find itself with obsolete inventory.

The EOQ formula was used for many years as the basis for an inventory that contained the smallest possible dollar investment. Prior to the advent of computer systems, it was the most comprehensive and understandable way to manage the inventory investment. However, that changed when advanced manufacturing systems appeared, as will be outlined later in this chapter. These systems can now calculate the precise demand for component parts, so that the purchasing staff can order the exact quantities needed for specific production periods. However, many companies are too small to make demands on their suppliers to ship quantities that do not match standard supplier shipment quantities. Consequently, the purchasing staff may have to use EOQ order quantities or at least the next largest standard shipment sizes allowed by suppliers, rather than the precise quantities outlined by whatever manufacturing planning system is in use. Thus, despite the advent of immensely more sophisticated manufacturing planning systems, there may still be a limited role for the EOQ model in today's corporation.

Production Schedule

The previous discussion noted how the EOQ concept is being partially supplanted by two alternative forms of manufacturing planning, which are detailed at the end of this chapter. However, before we delve into these two systems, it is important to understand the three underlying sets of information on which they are based. The first, which we have already covered, is the inventory database. The next, the production schedule, is covered in this section, followed by the bill of materials, which is described in the next section.

The production schedule is well described by its name. It is a listing of the quantities of subassemblies and finished goods that will be produced each day by a manufacturing facility. It is made up of a combination of customer orders and forecasted quantities for which there are not yet any customer orders. An example of such a schedule is shown in Figure 5.7.

Figure 5.7 contains two schedules. The first is a listing of the grand total quantities that will be manufactured in each period, sorted by product. The detailed group of forecasts and customer orders that comprise each production quantity are shown in the schedule. In the example, the second schedule lists only the forecasts and orders for a single week for one product. Part of the scheduled production

Figure 5.7

Sample Production Schedule

Production Schedule Summary

Part Number	Description	Week				
		1	2	3	4	5
09852-BLK	Bike, Racing, Black	150	25	75	45	200
09852-WHT	Bike, Racing, White	50	175	125	55	200
09511-BLU	Bike, Mtn, Blue	45	65	80	30	150
09511-WHT	Bike, Mtn, White	35	50	45	40	150
09221-MAU	Bike, Kid, Mauve	80	75	50	0	125
09221-MAG	Bike, Kid, Magenta	70	90	40	120	125

Production Schedule Detail, Week 1

Part Number	Description	Forecasts	Customer Orders	Customer Name	Customer Order No.	Customer Due Date
09852-BLK	Bike, Racing, Black	10		Sales Dept.	None	None
			20	Wheels Inc.	1247	3/4
			25	Sprocket	87321	3/5
			10	Smith Co.	22886	3/6
			50	Davis Bikes	1280	3/6
			35	Handle Bike	77491	3/7
	Totals	10	140			

includes a forecast, which is generated by the sales department. The sales staff adds this to the production schedule when it believes that there will be a number of purchases on short notice by customers. For weeks that are farther off in the future, there tends to be a large proportion of sales forecasts and only a small proportion of customer orders. Then, as actual orders come in, the sales staff continues to monitor its forecast and reduces the forecasted quantities. In the week of production, there is generally only a small proportion of forecasted quantities. The forecast is a very necessary component of the production schedule, because it gives the purchasing staff advance warning that component parts with long lead times must be purchased. If a company created a production schedule that contained nothing but customer orders, most of which are short-term, then the purchasing staff would not have a sufficient amount of warning to buy additional parts and would be forced to pay rush freight charges for some items.

The remainder of the sources of the sample production schedule are customer orders, which are due at the customers on specific dates listed on the right side of the report. A production scheduler may also introduce a third source of orders besides the forecast or customer order, which is the firm planned order. This is usually a clustering of customer orders into a single order that supersedes the customer orders and may include somewhat higher or lower quantities at the scheduler's option.

The production schedule is an excellent way to summarize all possible reasons for manufacturing a product into a time-sequenced report. Even without one of the manufacturing planning systems that will be described later in this chapter, it is extremely useful by itself for the production scheduling staff, for whom it is the primary working document.

A manufacturing planning system will use the production schedule in combination with information in the inventory and bill of material databases to schedule the flow of purchases, materials, and production through a facility. In the next section, we review the last of these key sources of information—the bill of materials.

Bill of Materials

One of a company's most important databases is its bills of material (BOMs). It is a key component of the manufacturing planning systems described later in this chapter, which are key to maintaining low inventory and high customer service levels.

A BOM is a listing of all the component parts that are used to manufacture a product. It lists the description and part number of each part, as well as the scrap rate for each one and any subassemblies that go into its manufacture. For more advanced manufacturing resource planning systems (discussed later in this chapter), it may also contain the sequence and time of usage for all machines involved in its manufacture. An example of a BOM is shown in Figure 5.8.

FIGURE 5.8

Sample Bill of Materials for a Camera

Part Number	Description	Unit of Measure	Part Quantity
NI-15002	Camera casing	Each	1.00
NI-15003	Viewfinder	Each	1.00
NI-15004	Winding lever	Each	1.00
NI-15005	Electronics subassembly	Each	1.00
NI-15006	Film holder	Each	1.00
NI-15007	Electronic flash	Each	1.00
NI-15008	Film advance readout	Each	2.00

Note in the example that there is a subassembly for electronic components. This refers to a second BOM that details the components of the subassembly. This is used whenever there are subassemblies used by multiple products, since it is easier to maintain a list of parts in just one BOM, rather than separately in many BOMs.

A BOM is used in a variety of ways. The most common one is as a pick list for the warehouse staff. When the materials handling personnel in the warehouse see that a product is about to be produced, they print a modified BOM called a "pick list," which they use to pick the correct parts from stock for the production run. In a more advanced form, the pick list will multiply the unit quantities on the BOMs by the unit quantities listed on the production schedule to yield a grand total quantity for each part that must be picked, as well as the warehouse location code where each part can be found. The report may also be sorted in order of warehouse location, so that pickers can use it to travel the shortest possible distance while picking parts. An example of such a pick list is shown in Figure 5.9, which uses as its basis the BOM noted in Figure 5.8.

Note that the pick list in Figure 5.9 contains a final column in which the stock picker writes the quantity actually picked. Because the required amount may not actually be in stock, this space is needed for the warehouse staff to record the amount that they will then enter into the computer system as having been picked for production purposes.

FIGURE 5.9

Sample Pick List for a Quantity of 200 Cameras

Location	Part No.	Description	U/M	Required Quantity	Quantity Picked
A-10-B	NI-15002	Camera casing	Each	200.00	198
A-14-C	NI-15003	Viewfinder	Each	200.00	200
A-18-D	NI-15004	Winding lever	Each	200.00	195
B-02-A	NI-15005	Electronics subassembly	Each	200.00	200
B-06-D	NI-15006	Film holder	Each	200.00	200
B-12-B	NI-15007	Electronic flash	Each	200.00	150
C-04-A	NI-15008	Film advance readout	Each	400.00	400

Yet another use of the BOM is by a material requirements planning system (described in detail in the next section). This system multiplies the BOMs by the production schedule to arrive at the total number of parts needed for production, less the amount already in stock, which is used by the purchasing staff to order the correct quantities of raw materials.

It is exceedingly important to maintain a very high degree of accuracy within a BOM. Since it is used for so many purposes, an error here can cause a multitude of problems in other parts of the company. For example, if the wrong part is listed on a BOM, the material requirements planning system will tell the purchasing staff to buy it, even though it will never be used. This increases the investment in inventory. Similarly, not including a part in a BOM will result in its not being available for production, which will halt the manufacturing process and delay delivery of completed products to customers. In addition, an incorrect quantity on the BOM will be translated into the pick list, which the warehouse staff will use to pick an incorrect quantity of parts from stock and deliver to the production staff, which will either have too many or too few parts, which in turn will require immediate corrective action. Thus, an inaccurate BOM results in problems in the warehouse, production, and purchasing areas, all of which contribute to poor customer service.

Material Requirements Planning

As computers became more powerful and lower in price, many of the inventory-related calculations that were previously computed by hand could now be automatically processed in moments, resulting in a new system that could balance the contradictory goals of lower inventory and higher customer service. It was initially called material requirements planning (MRP), though other features were later added to it to derive a more advanced system, called manufacturing resource planning. This later version is described in the next section.

An MRP system conducts its calculations with the assistance of three information sources, all of which have been described earlier in this chapter. The first is the production schedule, which it combines with the BOM for each item on the production schedule to determine the total amount of parts needed to produce each item on the schedule. It then checks the inventory database to see if any of the parts are currently in stock. If so, then it subtracts the on-hand inventory from the required quantity to arrive at a net amount of each part to be either purchased or produced, which it prints out as a schedule for the production and purchasing staffs to use. Though there are a number of other features, those steps are the essence of what MRP does—it breaks down a production schedule into all required parts that are not currently on hand, which the company then uses to schedule its purchasing and manufacturing.

With an MRP system in place, a company no longer has to keep excess quantities of any inventory on hand, since it knows precisely what parts are needed for all scheduled production. This means that it can eliminate all other inventory that the MRP system is not listing as being required for current production. By using this information, a company can reduce its inventory investment, which is one of the two inventory-related goals noted at the top of this chapter. Also, by providing complete detail regarding the parts needed to achieve the production schedule (which includes all customer orders), a company can improve its chances of shipping all required orders to customers and in a timely manner. This achieves the second goal, that of improving customer service. Further, even if a company is unable to produce on time, the MRP system will note the problem as far in advance as possible, so that the customer can be contacted and informed of a later delivery date before it becomes an inconvenience to the customer. Thus, the advent of computer systems that bring together disparate manufacturing information can now allow a company to reduce its inventory investment as well as provide its customers with better service.

To expand upon the initial explanation of MRP, it also involves timing. When the system calculates parts usage from the production schedule, it does not just break down the total number of component parts, less on-hand inventories, and stop. Instead, it extracts from a file called the "item master" the number of days of lead time required for a supplier to deliver each purchased part. The item master contains descriptive information about every part that is either in inventory or contained within a BOM. Using this lead time information, the MRP system determines the exact date on which any purchased parts must be ordered. It will also extract from the item master the name of the preferred supplier who sells the company this part, and will then send to the purchasing staff a purchase order, already filled out with purchase quantities, due dates, and the name of the supplier, for its approval. In addition, it will reduce the amount of this order by the quantities on any outstanding purchase orders that have not yet been received. If approved, the system can send this purchase order to the supplier over the Internet, by electronic data interchange, or by mail.

In addition to timing issues, an MRP system will also batch together part quantities from several days of scheduled production into a single purchase order, if required by users, since this will reduce the number of purchase orders sent to suppliers. More importantly, the item master can list either the EOQ or any ordering quantity specified by a user, which the MRP system will then include in its supplier orders for purchased parts. This may be necessary to avoid the freight or packaging costs associated with extremely small or odd-sized order quantities.

In addition to timing issues and order quantities, an MRP system can recognize the existence of subassemblies within a BOM, which usually calls for advance production of the subassemblies prior to the manufacture of the final product. It can schedule these within the production schedule, so that the manufacturing staff knows how many subassemblies to build and when they must be completed.

Though an MRP system has powerful scheduling capabilities that are beyond the abilities of any clerical staff, there are also some problems associated with it. They are as follows:

- *Required computing power.* An MRP system requires an inordinate amount of computing power. For example, if the system is decomposing a relatively small production schedule of 200 products into its component parts, it must search through the BOM for each one, as well as review the inventory records to see if parts are already available. Consequently, if each product contains an average of 50 parts, the MRP processing will require 20,000 transactions (which is calculated as 200 products times 50 parts equals 10,000 transactions, plus one extra transaction for each item, to check the on-hand inventory for parts). Though today's computers can process far more calculations than this per second, these are not just *calculations*—each one requires a disk access to check on a record in the manufacturing database, which is much more time consuming. Also, some systems will review an entire file from top to bottom to search for a single record, which exponentially increases the processing time, rather than using a more efficient indexing system to go straight to the required records. As a result, a complex MRP system may still require eight hours to process all updates. Since the MRP system is not available for use during this time, it can be a major burden for those companies that operate around the clock.

- *Impact of upstream changes.* Because an MRP system is so closely tied to the timing of transactions, changes to the production schedule in the very near term will result in major transaction changes and warnings to many system users. For example, if the production schedulers alter a scheduled production date from three weeks from now to tomorrow, the system will look to see if the required parts are available. If not, it will send urgent messages to the purchasing staff to order parts on a rush basis, for delivery tomorrow. To keep this from happening, a company that uses MRP must freeze the scheduling of all near-term production. The point at which changes to the production schedule are allowed should roughly correspond to the average lead time for purchased parts. For example, if most items can be obtained from suppliers within

10 days, then the schedule can be altered for all dates later than 10 days in the future.

- *Accuracy of underlying databases.* An MRP system is highly dependent on the accuracy of the underlying databases of manufacturing information. For example, if the system is told that there is a quantity of 10 items on hand and 10 are needed for immediate production, then the manufacturing department will grind to a halt if there are really only nine parts on hand. Similarly, if a BOM does not include a key part, then the MRP system will not know that it should buy the part. For these reasons, a company should adopt *minimum* accuracy standards of 95 percent for inventory and 98 percent for BOMs.

- *Required training.* An MRP system is a very complex one to operate, and so requires only the most skilled system operators. Because there are so many linked files in an MRP system, an operator problem in one area will cause a range of issues in other parts of the company that are difficult to correct. For example, if the sales staff incorrectly shifts the date of a forecast forward to the current date, the MRP system will assume that parts must be purchased right away and will inundate the purchasing staff with rush order notices. Also, if the engineers change the components in a BOM without telling anyone, the purchasing staff will also find itself being asked to buy new parts and cancel old ones, and possibly on a rush basis. For these reasons, a company must invest heavily in initial and ongoing training for all system users.

We will now proceed through a simple MRP example to illustrate how the system works. The MRP process begins with the production schedule. We will extract a single line item from the production schedule sample that was listed earlier in Figure 5.7. We will use the scheduled production in week 4 for part number 09511-BLU, which is a blue mountain bike. The quantity to be produced is 30 units. The MRP system then goes to the BOM of the blue mountain bike and multiplies 30 units by the BOM to determine the total number of parts required to build the bike. This calculation is shown in Figure 5.10.

In Figure 5.10, the BOM format, as noted earlier in Figure 5.8, is followed for the first four columns. Then we add the total production quantity for the mountain bike in the fifth column, which is 30 units.

FIGURE 5.10

Calculation of Parts Requirements for Mountain Bike Job

Part No.	Description	Unit of Measure	Part Quantity	Production Quantity	Total Parts Required
2357	Wheel	Each	2.000	30	60.000
2479	Tire	Each	2.000	30	60.000
2201	Front sprocket	Each	1.000	30	30.000
2509	Rear sprocket	Each	1.000	30	30.000
2642	Brake set	Each	1.000	30	30.000
2784	Front reflector	Each	1.000	30	30.000
2807	Rear reflector	Each	1.000	30	30.000
2110	Blue paint	Gallon	.125	30	3.750

We then multiply the part quantity in column 4 by the production quantity in column 5 to obtain the total number of parts required, which is shown in the final column.

The total required number of parts must now be netted against available inventory to determine how many more parts must be built or purchased. This portion of the example calculation is shown in Figure 5.11, where we have copied forward the part number and descrip-

FIGURE 5.11

Calculation of Part Quantities to Be Purchased for Mountain Bike Job

Part No.	Description	Total Parts Required	Unallocated Inventory	Unallocated Purchase Orders	Net Parts Required
2357	Wheel	60.000	15.000	10.000	35.000
2479	Tire	60.000	60.000	0.000	0.000
2201	Front sprocket	30.000	100.000	0.000	0.000
2509	Rear sprocket	30.000	0.000	0.000	30.000
2642	Brake set	30.000	8.000	5.000	17.000
2784	Front reflector	30.000	28.000	0.000	2.000
2807	Rear reflector	30.000	28.000	0.000	2.000
2110	Blue paint	3.750	1.000	1.000	1.750

FIGURE 5.12

Calculation of Purchasing Dates and Quantities for Mountain Bike Job

Part No.	Description	Manufacturing Due Date	Purchasing Lead Time	Required Order Date	Net Parts Required	Standard Ordering Quantity
2357	Wheel	3/3/2000	7	2/24/2000	35.000	50.000
2509	Rear sprocket	3/3/2000	7	2/24/2000	30.000	50.000
2642	Brake set	3/3/2000	9	2/22/2000	17.000	10.000
2784	Front reflector	3/3/2000	9	2/22/2000	2.000	5.000
2807	Rear reflector	3/3/2000	9	2/22/2000	2.000	5.000
2110	Blue paint	3/3/2000	2	3/1/2000	1.750	1.000

tion from Figure 5.10, as well as the number of total parts required for each item. We now add columns that list the total unallocated on-hand inventory for each item, as well as the total unallocated parts that are already on order. Most purchase orders are for parts that are already allocated to specific jobs, since there would otherwise be little point in buying them. However, it is common to have a residual quantity on a purchase order that is not allocated, because the purchasing department may be rounding up its orders to the next standard purchasing quantity or using an EOQ either approach will result in some unallocated purchases. We are interested in only the total unallocated quantities, since any parts that are already consigned to other jobs cannot be used for the production run of 30 mountain bikes. The final column notes the net quantity that must be purchased.

Having calculated the quantities of all parts that must be purchased, we now determine the dates when the purchases must be made, as well as the quantities to purchase. This calculation is shown in Figure 5.12 where we list the date when parts should be on hand for production and subtract out the number of days of lead time required by the supplier, which gives us the date on which the purchasing staff must place an order for the part. A good MRP system will also calculate the presence of weekends and add two extra days to a required order placement date if the date would otherwise fall on a weekend, when there is no one on hand to place the order. The table also notes the minimum number of parts required, which was taken from the last table, and lists next to it the standard ordering quantity, which the purchasing staff uses to determine the correct ordering quantity. The EOQ can be substituted for the standard ordering quantity.

Note that there are fewer line items in Figure 5.12 than in the preceding figures for the same example. This is because there is a sufficient quantity of two parts on hand, so that no purchases are required for them. An MRP system will present only action items to the purchasing staff, rather than inundate it with nonessential information about the other parts that are also required but are already on hand.

The example presents the essential calculations used by an MRP system. Though the size of the example was sharply curtailed, it is obvious from the number of calculations required that a production schedule of any size, coupled with even a few lengthy BOMs, will result in a highly complex series of calculations that requires extremely accurate data and complete understanding by a well-trained manufacturing and logistics staff to yield accurate results.

Manufacturing Resource Planning

The concept of manufacturing resource planning (MRP II) was developed as an extension of MRP. It uses the same concept of breaking down the production plan into its component parts to determine usage timing and quantities, except that this time we are not tracking materials, but rather the labor and machine capacity needed for production. To make MRP II work properly, there must be labor routings for each product. These are similar to a BOM in structure, except that they record the amount and type of labor needed to complete each product. The system then multiplies the production schedule by the labor routings for each of the items to be produced, which yields a listing required, and when they are needed. The production manager uses this information to staff the production operation properly, which may involve reducing or increasing the staff to match the planned production requirements. It is also very useful information for the production staff, which may find that the required labor for some products may so far exceed current staffing that the production schedule must be changed to reduce labor requirements. Alternatively, it may discover that the required labor hours will necessitate overtime or the addition of a shift, which it can then recommend to the production manager a week or more in advance, so that employees can be scheduled for this extra work.

The other aspect of MRP II is capacity planning. The system calculates the machine requirements for each phase of production of each item being manufactured, and summarizes this into a capacity report that lists the exact sequence and quantity of work that must be run through each machine. This information can be translated into reports for the operators of each workstation, who use it to schedule the sequence of their work for the day. The report also notes which machines will be overburdened with too much work, which the production scheduling staff uses to modify the production schedule to ensure that planned capacity usage does not exceed actual expectations. It is also possible to schedule preventive maintenance work into the production schedule, so that specific machines can be brought down for maintenance in an orderly manner that does not interfere with the production flow. Proper capacity planning is based on the accurate recording of machine time and sequence of machines used, which is usually recorded in the bill of materials for each product.

Both aspects of MRP II are extremely useful, especially for complex production flows that require the participation of a number of workstations before a product is completed. However, it also requires very accurate labor routings and BOMs to ensure that the reported labor and machine usage figures are correct. Consequently, the management team must arrange for a combination of feedback from the shop floor and audits by the industrial engineering staff to ensure that these figures are accurate.

Just-in-Time

The MRP and MRP II systems just described are based on a "push" system: The production scheduling staff determines what will be produced, based on a mix of customers orders and internal forecasts, and "pushes" production through the facility. This means that there is a surge of work-in-process inventory, which gradually works its way through the facility and eventually results in a group of finished goods in the warehouse that will (hopefully) be sold to customers if orders arrive. This approach can result in an excessive quantity of all kinds of inventory, because some of the production may not be founded upon actual customer orders, but rather on a supposition that orders will eventually arrive. Also, each machine in the production flow can create as many parts as the operator desires (within reason), so that excessive part quantities will flow out of some machines and build up in front of a downstream machine that operates at a slower production rate. This results in extra work-in-process. Finally, parts are ordered for the push system based in part on forecasts, which may exceed the quantity of actual orders received, so raw material quantities may also be too high. When this much extra inventory is on hand, there is not only a risk that it will never be used up, but also that the excess quantities can be damaged in storage, or that they mask quality defects that will not be discovered until they are eventually brought out of storage and inspected. To counteract all these problems, the just-in-time (JIT) manufacturing system was developed.

Under this system, the production flow is "pulled" from the shipping dock backwards through the facility. For example, if a customer places an order for a product, the JIT system will issue a production authorization card, called a *kanban,* to the last workstation in the production chain that creates the product. This workstation will find that it cannot operate without subsidiary-level parts from other workstations that are located earlier in the parts process, and so it will issue another set of kanban authorization cards to those workstations, allowing them to build exactly enough parts for the first workstation. If there are many production levels, then there may be quite a few kanban cards being sent backward through the production process. Finally, when the earliest workstation in the chain receives an authorization card, it builds the exact amount of product signified by the card and moves the completed product to the requesting workstation, along with the card. The earliest workstation is not allowed to complete any other work until it receives another authorization card. By using this process, none of the workstations in a production facility can produce any extra parts beyond those specifically needed to assemble a product for a customer order.

This seemingly simple process flow has enormous ramifications. First, it orients a production facility in the direction of very short production run quantities, possibly as few as one at a time. This is a difficult transition to make if a facility is made up of large machines that require lengthy setups to convert to the production of different parts, which is why such machines typically have lengthy production runs to justify the time and cost of each machine setup. To avoid this problem, the engineering staff must focus on the processes surrounding machine changeovers, usually with the assistance of a videotape of the process, which they review repeatedly to eliminate all unnecessary steps. After many iterations, a typical machine setup time can be reduced to less than ten percent of the previous time period, which allows the production staff to quickly switch back and forth between the production of different parts. Another approach to this problem is to sell off a company's large and inflexible production machinery that is geared toward high production volumes, and replace them with smaller machines that can be switched over to different production configurations with greater speed. Either approach contributes to the use of very short production runs.

If a company shifts to rapid machine setups, this requires a more highly trained staff than was previously the case, since each machine operator must be skilled in the conversion process. Also, if many small machines replace a few large ones, then a natural consequence of this change is to group the smaller machines together and have a small number of employees either run several of them at once, or several in sequence. The sequential pattern is more common, in which employees stay in small "machine cells" of a half-dozen machines and walk a part through each machine in sequence. For these reasons, a company must shift to a more highly qualified workforce, which can either be the same one—but with intensive and continuing training—or a new and more highly skilled workforce.

Delivery quantities in a JIT system are much smaller and more frequent than is normally the case. This is because the philosophy behind the system is to keep raw material quantities as low as possible. To do this, the kanban concept is extended to suppliers, usually through an electronic or fax notification, that they must send small shipments to the production facility just in time for them to be used in the daily production process. Given the short notification time periods involved, this methodology generally restricts a company to the use of suppliers who are located very close to the production facility, since suppliers located farther away require excessively long notification lead times (so that they can transport the goods to the facility on time). This frequent delivery concept can be extended to having suppliers deliver parts straight to the specific machines that will need them, thereby avoiding the receiving process entirely.

If the short delivery concept is used, then there will be so many deliveries coming into the plant that the receiving staff will have difficulty reviewing everything on a timely basis and forwarding them to the various parts of the facility that need them. Also, if there is a quality problem with some of the parts, then the receiving staff must notify the supplier that it must deliver replacement parts immediately, which may cause a delay in the production process if the replacement parts are not delivered on time. To avoid both of these problems, the purchasing department can alter its job to include the qualification of suppliers, so that they are certified for having a production process that always results in parts of a high quality. By creating this certification process, a company can eliminate its receiving process, because it knows that all parts delivered will be in the correct quantities and will surpass minimum quality levels. The engineering department will usually be involved in this certification process too, since it has the requisite industrial engineering skills to verify that supplier production processes are sufficient.

Yet another result of the JIT approach is that the related paperwork changes considerably. For example, if suppliers bypass the receiving function and deliver straight to the production facility, then there is no verification system for ensuring that the parts were actually received. Also, the very high number of supplier deliveries will result in a very large number of supplier invoices, since they typically issue one invoice for each shipment. To avoid both of these problems, the accounting department can pay suppliers based on the number of parts used in its production process, which it determines by multiplying the number of products produced in a period by their BOMs, which reveals the number of parts used in the production period. For this approach to work, however, a company must also be able to track and pay suppliers for any additional parts it scraps, since these would otherwise not be revealed by the number of products manufactured. Also, because there is no supplier invoice, the accounting staff must add sales taxes for the jurisdictions in which suppliers are located to the periodic payments made to them.

Yet another issue is that most traditional management reporting systems are not necessary. For example, a traditional manufacturing system keeps close track of direct labor and machine utilization; however, this is useless in a JIT environment, since both utilization levels tend to be low. The emphasis under this system is on reduced inventory levels, rather than high utilization. Similarly, nearly all management reports related to production line problems are too slow to be useful, because the information on which they are based must be accumulated, summarized, and forwarded to the management team. Because production runs can be as small as one, the work has long since been completed by the time a manager shows up to discuss the issue. Instead, it is most useful to develop a rapid warning system, such as a red light over a machine, that an operator can turn on as soon as a problem develops, and which warns the maintenance staff to review the problem at once. Thus, there is little need for formal management reporting systems in a JIT environment.

We have thus far outlined many changes that must be made in all parts of a company in order to make a JIT system work properly—changes in machine sizes and layout, setup times, employee training, receiving procedures, purchasing patterns, and accounting paperwork. This system involves a fundamental change in the way a company operates. Is it worth the change? Let us first return to the two goals outlined at the beginning of this chapter.

A JIT system is the best one yet devised for reducing a company's investment in inventory. At Toyota Motor Company, which originated the system, inventory turnover rates exceeding 70 are the norm. The system is particularly good at reducing raw material inventory, since JIT deliveries of small part quantities reduce this area to a vanishingly small amount. It has a similar impact on work-in-process inventory, because the kanban system is precisely targeted at the reduction of inventory buildups between machines (though some inventory can still accumulate in lesser quantities). It does not necessarily have an impact on finished goods inventory, because the sales department can still use forecasts that are not substantiated by actual customer orders to drive the JIT system to produce finished goods. The overall impact of this system on a company's inventory investment is extremely positive.

The JIT system also has a positive impact on customer service, for two reasons. First, the system has a tight focus on producing to specific orders, so it is difficult for a customer order to be lost by this system. Also, because parts are individually inspected by machine operators as they travel through the system, quality problems are found and corrected immediately; therefore, customers rarely have a reason to complain about quality problems in the finished goods they receive.

Despite the obvious benefits of a JIT system, any management team that is considering its implementation must also consider a number of problems with it, including:

- *Employee resistance.* For those employees who have grown up with more traditional manufacturing systems that "push" production through a production facility, the use of kanbans, short production runs, quick changeovers, revised paperwork and reporting systems, and manufacturing cells seems to be absolutely alien and inherently not the "right" way to do things. These employees may not be just production line workers, but also senior level managers, whose way of life has revolved around the old systems. These people are likely to oppose a JIT system, or at least not support it, and can be one of the main reasons why a JIT installation fails.
- *Supplier difficulties.* A properly functioning JIT system depends to some extent on on-time deliveries in small quantities by suppliers who are certified to ship directly to specific machines within the facility and who have agreed to be paid based on parts usage in finished production. These are advanced concepts for suppliers to grasp, and some may not be willing to agree to them, especially if a company is a small one and has no leverage with its suppliers in terms of purchasing volume.
- *Machinery reconfiguration.* A company that has made a major investment in very large and automated machinery must justify the expense with long and very efficient production runs, which is the reverse strategy advocated under the JIT system. For these

companies to switch over to short production runs with such large equipment will require large changeover costs, which may not make the JIT system cost effective. Because the best option for such companies is to replace their large equipment with smaller and more flexible equipment, the cost of doing so may keep them from experimenting with the approach.

- *Training issues.* The JIT system treats the entire manufacturing concept in a different manner from the one that most employees have seen for their entire working lives, and so they will have trouble adjusting to the new process. It takes a great deal of repetitive training at all levels of an organization to overcome this problem. If a company does not invest in JIT training, then the conversion to this system will probably fail.
- *Accounting system modifications.* A particularly thorny problem is that most accounting departments process their transactions using the systems built into their packaged accounting software, which require supplier invoices and receiving documentation before payments to suppliers are allowed. Under the JIT system, there may be no supplier invoices, with payments being calculated from production records instead, nor will there be any receiving documentation, because most deliveries go straight to the production floor and bypass the receiving dock. Consequently, the accounting staff must bypass or modify its "canned" accounting software to create new systems that will handle the altered paper flow of a JIT system.

Many companies have found the problems outlined here to be formidable ones, resulting in either failed or only partially successful JIT system installations. To improve the odds of installing a JIT system, it is highly advisable to hire a group of consultants who have experience with such system installations, so that they can guide a company through problem areas. Also, there must be a very strong emphasis on the training of all employees, from senior management through the direct labor staff, regarding how the system works. The training can also be conducted by the consultants, since they speak from experience. Finally, there must be an absolute commitment to the system by the management team, for it cannot waffle and attempt to return to the previous system, just because a few bugs have cropped up during the JIT installation process. If a company follows these guidelines, it can successfully install a system that greatly reduces its inventory investment while providing excellent customer service.

The Differences between MRP and JIT Systems

Having just reviewed two very different manufacturing systems, one may wonder which is the correct method to use. In this section, we compare the MRP and JIT systems, contrasting specific features of the two systems. They are as follows:

- *Computer usage.* An MRP system requires a great deal of computing power to operate properly. This includes an MRP software package, the best of which cost several million dollars, plus a mini-computer or even a mainframe on which to run it. A JIT system, however, can theoretically avoid a computer entirely, though in actuality a low-end computer system is of considerable use for the storage of BOM information about products being manufactured.
- *Database accuracy.* An MRP system requires superior levels of accuracy in its inventory, BOM, and production scheduling databases, as well as its labor routing and capacity planning files if the system is upgraded to an MRP II system. The calculated results issued by this system will otherwise contain too many inaccuracies to make the system usable. A JIT system, however, requires only an accurate BOM database. There is no need for any inventory database, because the system assumes that there is no inventory kept on hand.
- *Inventory investment.* An MRP system requires a larger inventory investment than a JIT system, for it assumes the storage of some raw materials inventory, and it is more likely that some work-in-process inventory will build up between the machines, since an MRP system does not focus as closely as JIT on the reduction of in-process materials.
- *Machine setups.* An MRP system assumes that machine setup times will remain the same, whereas a JIT system continually pursues ever-shorter setup times. If a company chooses to reduce its setup times in an MRP environment, the MRP software can take these

changes into account, but the system does not focus on improving this item.

- *Paperwork.* An MRP system issues a great deal of paper. There are production schedules, shop floor reports, scrap reports, and variance reports. A JIT system has virtually no paperwork besides an initial production schedule, which is frequently driven by nothing more than a batch of customer orders. However, the most sophisticated JIT systems will issue electronic bulletins to suppliers, notifying them of when to send deliveries and what should be contained in them.

- *Quality.* The quality of parts produced by a JIT system are almost always better than those coming from an MRP system. The reason for the difference is that, by striving for zero work-in-process inventory in a JIT system, parts will flow between workstations so fast that the downstream workstations will spot problems in parts they receive before upstream workstations have a chance to build any more defective ones. Because of this immediate feedback loop, it is very difficult for a JIT system to create low-quality parts.

- *Training.* Both systems require extensive personnel training. Under an MRP system, the level of training must be particularly high for the production scheduling and purchasing staffs, who are heavy system users.

Based on the comparisons noted here, it is evident that a well-run JIT system will produce better results than an MRP system in most respects. However, note that the JIT system must be *well run.* As noted in the preceding section, JIT systems are difficult to install, and so a company switching from an MRP to a JIT system may find that improvements will be hard to find until the new system is thoroughly installed and all operating errors flushed out.

For those companies already operating an MRP system, a halfway measure is to adopt some of the JIT principles and incorporate them into the existing system. For example, material receipts can bypass the receiving dock by qualifying supplier processes, while supplier deliveries can be made more frequently and in smaller quantities. Similarly, there is no reason why machine setup times cannot be reduced and run lengths shortened in an MRP environment. Completing these steps will improve the results posted by an MRP system, though the results will not match those of a JIT system.

Summary

We have demonstrated in this chapter that the key to reducing a company's inventory investment while also attaining a high degree of customer service is the use of precise manufacturing planning systems that are geared to produce to the exact requirements of customers. To make these complex systems work well, a company must focus on creating and maintaining highly accurate databases for inventory, production schedules, and bills of material. Only by keeping accuracy levels very high in all three areas can a company operate a manufacturing system that maintains just enough inventory to create products for customers on the dates and in the quantities they request.

Chapter 6

Outsourcing Selected Company Functions

As a company grows, the business owner may find that the plethora of new functions that are a necessary part of a large business are too much to handle—taxes to be filed; products to manufacture; computer systems to install, maintain, and upgrade; and so on. The management of so many functions can reduce a company's initially tight focus on a specific strategic direction, such as client advertising needs, rolling out a line of restaurants, or conducting new medical research. Instead, manager meetings become bogged down in other matters, such as the installation of a new telephone system, problems with issuing invoices to customers, or quality problems with the janitorial staff. If this appears to be a problem, the answer may be to outsource selected company functions, which allows management to return to its earlier focus on strategic issues.

In this chapter, we review the reasons why a company should (and should not) consider outsourcing, and how to select a supplier to whom functions can be outsourced, as well as how to transition the data, staff, and processes over to that supplier. We then delve into the best ways to manage and control the activities of a supplier, and finish with a review of the reasons both in favor of and against the outsourcing of specific functional areas. By the end of this chapter, the reader should have a good concept of the advantages and dangers of outsourcing, as well as how to make the concept succeed in practice.

The Strategy of Outsourcing

There are a number of good reasons for outsourcing certain company functions, as well as risks that one must weigh before making the decision to do so. In this section, we review the most common reasons favoring outsourcing and balance this discussion with a commentary on the most typical outsourcing problems.

One of the best reasons to engage in outsourcing is to acquire new skills. This is particularly important for those functional areas that require considerable experience and training, such as accounting, computer services, and engineering. The types of skills needed may be of the technical or managerial variety. This reason is brought up most frequently by the managers of older companies that have found their competitive skills to be significantly lower than those of the competition, and wish to upgrade those skills rapidly by bringing in the services of a supplier who is skilled in a particular function, and who has experience in implementing all the latest procedures and technological advances. Another reason why a company may outsource to acquire new skills is not that it has antiquated systems, but rather that there has been a long history of departmental inefficiency, which is usually caused by either poor management or weak employee hiring or training practices. Bringing in fresh new skills through an outsourcing deal can resolve these problems.

Another reason to engage in outsourcing is that the management team wants to focus the bulk of its time on only those activities that will contribute to the advancement of the company's strategic direction. This reasoning arises most frequently when a company is just starting up and has few managers on hand to manage many functions, or when the existing management staff is weak and the time of the few good managers must not be squandered on nonessential activities. Companies operating under this philosophy tend to outsource functions that require fewer skills, such as janitorial, administrative, and maintenance functions, since they are purposely reserving the high-end, value-added functions, such as engineering and computer services, for themselves.

For those companies with either cash flow problems or a tight focus on improving cash flow, another reason for resorting to outsourcing is that it can reduce or eliminate investments in either capital expenditures or staffing. This is because the supplier may conduct operations out of its own facility, and will do so with its own staff. It may even be possible to sell assets to a supplier that are related to the outsourced function, since they will no longer be needed by the company; this immediately frees up cash for other purposes that may be more central to key company operations.

Yet another reason to use outsourcing is that it can assist a rapidly growing company that does not have the time to develop a fully integrated set of corporate functions. For example, a start-up software company may begin with a reasonably good set of software engineers but has neither the time nor the inclination to also hire managers and staff for the advertising, accounting, or computer services departments. These companies need to bring in a fully operational department immediately, and one that is sufficiently scalable to ensure that it can handle rapid increases in transactional demands. Given their expertise, the larger outsourcing suppliers are able to fulfill these requirements.

A company may find that its sales volume is highly seasonal, which creates undue pressure on the staffs of many departments that must handle this volume, such as accounting, customer service, and production. If so, a good reason to adopt outsourcing is that a company can retain a small staff that is proficient in transacting a minimal level of business all year, while an outsourcing supplier handles all of the overflow traffic. This is a particularly effective solution in the customer service area, where overflow calls can be instantly routed to regional call centers that are operated by inbound telemarketing suppliers. This approach keeps a company from having to invest in the hiring and training of temporary personnel who will be let go after the prime selling season has been completed.

In a small number of situations, a start-up company may want to adopt the outsourcing of one or two key functions to a major and well-known supplier, so that it can market the outsourcing relationship to its customers as a major benefit of working with the company.

For example, it may outsource its logistics to Ryder Logistics, or its computer services function to Andersen Consulting or EDS, which gives the company the cachet of association with organizations that are famed for their skill. This may even extend to creating presentations to customers that include members of the outsourcing suppliers as part of the presentation team.

A final reason for using outsourcing is that there are some situations in which outsourcing can save money. This is most common when the supplier can conduct services from a highly efficient central location that it operates on behalf of a number of its customers, which allows it to cut costs through the centralization of staff and management, as well as the increased efficiencies related to centralized processes and computer systems. For example, this can apply to a centralized truck maintenance center, a single data processing center, or a large inbound or outbound telemarketing call center. Thus, this option applies mostly to the minority of outsourcing situations in which services can be performed from a supplier site, not at the company location.

Against this imposing list of reasons favoring the use of outsourcing are an equally large array of problems that can arise when outsourcing is used. When a manager is considering the move to outsourcing, it is extremely important to give considerable weight to the following issues that may make outsourcing not only an expensive proposition, but also the strategically incorrect way to run a business.

- *Cost.* In most cases, outsourcing is more expensive than the cost of conducting the same services within the company with an internal staff. The reason for the costing disparity is that the supplier has additional advertising and marketing costs that the internal department does not have to incur, plus the supplier's profit margin; because the internal department is probably a cost center, it does not mark up its services with a profit margin. Also, in the case of activities that require highly skilled employees, such as accounting, computer services, or engineering, the internal cost per employee hour is far lower than the rate billed by most suppliers, simply because the marketplace places a very high premium on these value-added services. For example, the internal cost of a computer programmer may be only $30 per hour, whereas the hourly fee for the same person who is employed by a supplier is probably in excess of $100. This is the single largest shock to most business owners, who jump on the popular outsourcing band-wagon, only to find that service from the function has not changed much, but that its cost has appreciably increased.

- *Loss of capability.* A particularly dangerous problem is that a company will probably dismantle its in-house capability once it has shifted a function to a supplier, which gives it very little chance to throw out the supplier (in the event of poor performance) and restart its internal operations. This is a particular problem for those functions requiring employees with the highest level of skill and experience, since these departments require years to assemble and mold into a smoothly running operation.

- *Management.* Once a company has outsourced a function, the management team should not assume that the function will now magically run itself without any further oversight. On the contrary, there must be a manager assigned to each supplier, one who is responsible for measuring the supplier's performance, maintaining control over the quality of its work, and approving all bills submitted. Only through such continuous oversight can the management team be assured that outsourced functions are being run in an efficient and effective manner. However, the level of management oversight may surprise the management team that originally decided to outsource precisely because it wanted to spend more management time on other issues.

- *Loss of sponsor.* When a company decides to outsource a function, it is usually because there is a sponsor within the management team who is backing the concept, and who ensures funding and other forms of support as the outsourcing continues. If this person leaves the company or is in any way unable to continue offering support, then the outsourcing arrangement may fail due to a reduced level of attention, or because the sponsor's replacement prefers the more traditional approach of keeping all functions in-house. When this happens, there will be a significant cost associated with shifting away from the supplier, as well as transactional problems that inevitably arise when responsibility for completing work is shifted to a different group of people.

Clearly, there are many good reasons to consider outsourcing as a viable approach for running some parts of a company. However, there are also many risks associated with outsourcing a function. Consequently, the management team usually follows a progression, such as the one shown in Figure 6.1, in which only the simplest functions are outsourced. Then the management team learns how to negotiate contracts with suppliers, as well as how to control and manage them, which gives it a better comfort level with the outsourcing concept. It then gradually moves into the outsourcing of more complex functions that may be more closely intertwined with the company's strategic direction. As noted in the example, this means that such areas as janitorial or maintenance services are outsourced first, followed by support functions such as customer service or accounting. Last of all

FIGURE 6.1

The Typical Outsourcing Path

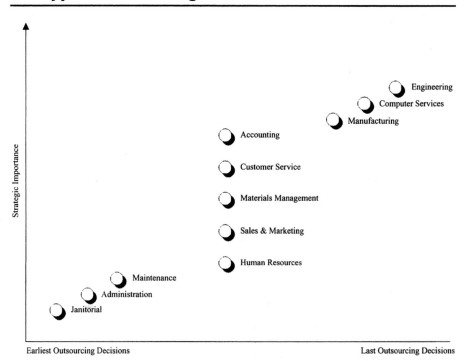

Source: Steven Bragg, *Outsourcing* (New York: John Wiley & Sons, 1998), p. 6. Reprinted with permission.

come the functions in which a company feels it generates its greatest value, and which involves the greatest levels of employee skill and competence. These are usually the computer services, manufacturing, and engineering functions.

The shift to outsourcing is an important decision, especially for the most crucial functional areas, as noted previously in Figure 6.1. Given the risks of failure, it is best for the management team to carefully and slowly proceed through the remaining steps of selecting and transitioning to a supplier (as described in the next two sections) in as thoughtful and orderly a manner as possible, in order to ensure that the team makes the right decision.

Selecting a Supplier

The first step in selecting a supplier is to obtain a list of potential candidates. Many of the nationally recognized suppliers advertise through the outsourcing directory that is published by The Outsourcing Institute, located in Brooklyn, New York. This organization also organizes lengthy outsourcing advertisements in most of the major business magazines, and sponsors a number of outsourcing seminars around the country. Another source is advertisements in industry trade journals, such as *Computer World, Information Week,* or *Logistics.* The bulk of outsourcing services can be obtained through local suppliers who advertise in the Yellow Pages. This is one of the best sources of supplier references for maintenance, janitorial services, and payroll processing.

The second step is to determine a list of requirements that the company wants to have its future outsourcing supplier fulfill. This may seem like a simple matter—"I want them to take over the computer services department!"—but does this include hardware and software maintenance, help desk staffing, software version upgrades, programming, and legacy system maintenance? Some additional analysis may reveal that management wants to outsource only a small portion of a function and keep the rest. Also, there may be specific tasks within a function that are of extreme importance to management. To use the same example, management may require skilled programming assistance more than anything, in which case it should assign an especially high weighting to this task.

Once the company has developed a written list of outsourcing requirements, it should integrate the list into a formal request for proposals (RFP) document that will be sent to suppliers as part of the next step in the selection process. Additional points that should be covered by the RFP are:

- Familiarization information about the company's industry.
- The scope of the outsourcing work.
- The bid due date and final selection date.
- Information to be provided by the supplier in its response.
- The criteria the company will use to select a supplier.
- Pricing expectations.

The company then sends the RFP to all suppliers whom it has located, with a request to return the lists by a specified due date, having added to it a comprehensive set of documentation that describes each supplier's ability to meet each requirement. The responses should also include a half-dozen or more names of other companies who have outsourced their functions to the supplier, as well as supplier financial statements. Once the RFP due date has passed, the management team reviews and scores all supplier responses based on their ability to complete the requirements list, as well as their proposed pricing and financial condition. This is a situation in which a supplier's financial condition is of considerable importance, since the outsourcing relationship may well last for a decade or more, during which time the company must rely on the supplier to stay solvent while providing services to it. Of particular importance are the results of reference checks with the reference list turned in by each supplier. Those people assigned to conduct the interviews should always ask for the names of additional companies who use supplier services, because these additional ones (who were *not* referred to the company by the supplier) may not have received service at the same level as those who were originally referred. Examples of questions to cover during the reference calls are the operating style of the supplier, the extent of its add-on pricing, its level of staff and management experience, use of subcontractors, the level of responsiveness to complaints, issues requiring contract renegotiation, and the extent and nature of any disputes. The management team will then select the best supplier from the list, based on the closeness of its ability to meet the company's needs as specified in the RFP, plus its financial condition and the results of the discussions with references. This should be a thorough and considered process that is not rushed—selecting the wrong supplier can require a great deal of work in the future to correct.

Once the management team has selected a supplier, it must still negotiate a contract, which can be a difficult proposition for some types of outsourcing. For example, a contract to outsource the entire computer services department may be almost entirely unique to the deal, with very little "boilerplate" legal clauses, whereas a payroll outsourcing contract is usually just a form contract that is not subject to change, save for some variation in pricing. In general, the duration of contract negotiation is highest for the outsourcing of computer services and manufacturing. For these two areas in particular, one should be especially careful of the following contractual issues:

- *Issues to be deferred for postcontract resolution.* If a supplier tries to persuade management to sign a basic contract and conduct further negotiations over "a few small items" later on, this means that the supplier is attempting to legally lock in the company, sometimes for a multiyear period, which gives it more negotiating leverage over the remaining "few small items," since the company is obligated to honor the contract, and no longer has the option to walk away. When the management team sees this kind of negotiating behavior, it is likely that the same "hardball" negotiating tactics will be used for the duration of the contract, so it may be a wise move to cancel further negotiations and switch to the second most desirable outsourcing supplier.
- *Baseline fees.* The supplier will always try to include the smallest number of services in the monthly baseline service fee, which allows it to charge exorbitant rates on all other services on an incremental basis. To avoid this situation, a company should always strive for the reverse—the inclusion of all services, or as

many as possible, in a single baseline fee. Also, any increases in this fee should be tightly controlled in the contract; for example, an annual inflationary increase is allowed, but only up to a maximum amount, after which there is a hard cap on further annual increases.

- *Additional fees.* The supplier may also want a termination fee if the company cancels the contract earlier than the date specified in the contract. This may be a reasonable request, since the supplier may be making a capital investment in the company that will not be paid off until the end of the contract, or engaging in subcost pricing at the beginning of the contract, with higher pricing scheduled near the end of the contract. If this is the case, then management should review the supplier's calculations that back up its claim for termination fees, and agree to a reasonable figure based on these notes. The company can also be aggressive in the matter of additional fees. For example, it can request a switch to variable pricing, so that the supplier is paid based on the number of transactions processed, rather than a fixed fee per period. This approach allows a company to reduce the amount of its fixed costs, so that its breakeven point is lower.

- *Supplier contract boilerplate.* The supplier has structured its standard contract form to be entirely favorable to itself. Rather than have company lawyers pore through the document and fight over dozens of contractual terms, it is frequently easier to write a whole new contract, which is much more likely to have terms that are favorable to the company. Given the cost of dealing with an unfavorable contract over many years, it is much less expensive to invest up front in extra legal fees to write a new contract.

- *Undefined services.* A major problem for both the supplier and the company is that services to be provided by the supplier are not clearly defined in the contract. As a result, the supplier may bid too low, on the assumption that it is providing only a limited number of services, while the company's expectations are much higher, since it assumes that the supplier will be handling additional services. This can lead to considerable conflict over pricing issues after the contract has been signed and additional negotiations that may result in a less favorable price than was originally indicated by the supplier's bid price. Consequently, the contract should contain a very detailed list of activities and transaction quantities to be completed by the supplier.

- *Staff movement.* If a company is shifting some of its staff to a supplier as part of an outsourcing deal, then there is a risk that the supplier will move some of the best former company employees to other clients, which will create a risk of reduced efficiency in the newly outsourced function. To avoid this, the company should include in the contract a clause that allows it to retain the services of a number of specific supplier personnel, usually for a period of one or two years. This time period allows the supplier to train replacement personnel, who can take the place of any employees who are subsequently transferred elsewhere.
- *Termination causes.* A company may find that the supplier is not meeting performance expectations, but the contract does not allow it to terminate the outsourcing arrangement. To avoid this situation, the company should insist on a set of performance metrics that the supplier must meet, or else the company has legal cause to terminate the contract without penalty. It is reasonable to allow the supplier some period of time (such as 90 days) in which to improve its performance before the company is allowed to terminate the arrangement.

Even the best-written contract will sometimes be missing agreements that only come to light later, after the outsourcing arrangement has been in operation for some time. To avoid costly lawsuits over disagreements about the correct terms of these added agreements, the original contract should also include a provision for the use of an arbitrator, which improves the speed of contract changes while reducing their cost.

Though the large number of issues raised here may make a management team think that the legal hassles make outsourcing too difficult to initiate, it must understand that an outsourcing arrangement may last for many years, in which case the ground rules for how the two parties interact must be carefully defined prior to the commencement of the marriage.

Transitioning to a Supplier

Once the contract is signed, the work of the management team is by no means complete. It must now transition an in-house function to the supplier, which is rife with personnel, data, and systems problems. In this section, we review the steps to be followed for most outsourcing situations. The steps should be followed in the exact order listed, because the completion of later steps is highly dependent on the prior completion of earlier ones. They are as follows:

1. *Assign in-house responsibility for the supplier to a manager.* Once a function is handed over to a supplier, the company cannot assume that the supplier will handle the entire transition process by itself. On the contrary, it needs the assistance of a high-level manager who can push through all necessary transition changes. For example, if the engineering department is being outsourced, then the vice president of engineering should be the functional coordinator. Similarly, if any aspect of the accounting function is switching to a supplier, then the controller should be the functional coordinator.

2. *Break the news.* Those employees who are to be outsourced should be notified as soon in the process as possible, since rumors will be begin to fly as soon as the next step is initiated—and it is best to be as up-front and honest with employees as possible over such an issue that will affect their careers. This notification should be a formal meeting, at which the supplier should be present, and should run as long as necessary to answer all employee questions.

3. *Itemize the experience levels of all employees to be transferred.* The supplier needs to know how many of its existing staff must be brought in and how many of the current company staff can be retained on-site. The only way it can obtain this information is to review the experience and training records of all employees in the function that is to be outsourced. This should include staff interviews.

4. *Review processes.* The supplier needs to know exactly how the internal processes function within the area that is to be outsourced. This calls for interviews and flowcharting to verify business processes. The management team may require a confidentiality

agreement from the supplier at this point, since it may be delving into areas of the company that are considered confidential. This is essentially a due diligence phase in the transition process, so there may also be some contract renegotiation at this point in order to clarify legal issues or adjust contract pricing.

5. *Transfer documentation.* The supplier needs copies of all documentation used by the in-house staff that is being outsourced, such as policies and procedures, training manuals, and activity schedules. However, send only copies—the company may need the originals later on if the outsourcing deal falls through and it must return to the old operational system.

6. *Transfer fixed assets and personnel.* In a few cases, there may be a transfer of fixed assets, which calls for an audit of fixed asset identification numbers prior to the transfer. Also, representatives from the human resources departments of both companies should meet with all employees who are being transferred to the supplier, to ensure that all questions are answered and forms signed that are related to pay, benefits, and payroll deductions.

7. *Transfer operations.* The supplier now takes over responsibility for operations within the outsourced function. This is not a simple step, because it may involve a complex transfer of data to new computer systems, parallel operations by both parties for a short time, and numerous error corrections.

8. *Disposal of leftover assets.* Once the function has shifted to the supplier, there may be excess fixed assets or office space available, which the company can dispose of by the most advantageous means possible, which may include the sale of assets, the sublease of space, or the sale of entire buildings.

The transition steps listed here are only the most common ones encountered for the majority of outsourcing deals. In some cases, such as janitorial outsourcing, the transition steps are much simpler, whereas others, such as the outsourcing of computer services, are exceedingly complex and require an immensely detailed project plan to properly transition. In the most difficult cases, management should bring in a highly experienced group of project managers to handle the transition process.

Managing the Supplier

The primary step that a company can take to properly manage a supplier is to assign a manager to it, who treats it in precisely the same manner as he or she would if the supplier were a part of the company. This means that there should be continual measurement of the supplier's performance, with this information being acted on by the manager as well as presented to senior management. Also, the internal audit group should be scheduled for regular reviews of those parts of the supplier's operations that affect its outsourcing services to the company. In addition, there should be regularly scheduled planning and review meetings between the company's assigned manager and the supplier's representatives. The topics of these meetings should be the results of ongoing improvement plans, future planning, the most recent performance measurement results, and any other issues that have arisen and require resolution at this level. The amount of management involvement will be intense for the most critical areas, such as engineering and computer services, with correspondingly less management time allocated to those suppliers who are occupied with more mundane functional areas, such as maintenance.

In short, a company must maintain management control over its outsourcing suppliers to the same extent that it manages its internal functions. Though a company may believe that it is engaging in outsourcing in order to reduce the oversight work of the management team, this is not a goal that is completely achievable—some oversight must continue, to ensure that outsourced functions are still being operated in an efficient and effective manner.

Measuring the Supplier

A management team needs to know the exact performance level of all its outsourcing suppliers. To do this, it must establish a baseline set of measurements, determine the company's performance level prior to handing over operations to a supplier, and then continue to conduct measurements at periodic intervals after the supplier has taken over operations. By using these steps, one can compare ongoing supplier performance to the levels that the company experienced prior to outsourcing.

When creating a list of performance measurements, one must be careful to split them into two categories—one that tracks the maintenance of ongoing functions, and one that tracks the supplier's ability to improve operations. For example, a maintenance measurement in the accounting area would be the ability to issue all invoices to customers within one day of shipment. In the logistics area, this would be the ability to arrange for on-time truckload shipments that always arrive at the shipping dock at the scheduled hour. These are basic functional measurements that track the supplier's ability to manage the fundamental operations for which they are responsible. The second type of measurement tracks a supplier's ability to create value for a company. For example, in the accounting area, if a supplier could improve collections to the point where accounts receivable turns are doubled, this is a major improvement in operations and one that deserves recognition. In the logistics arena, such a measurement would be finished goods inventory turnover, since the supplier could greatly reduce a company's investment in this area through better distribution systems. It is important not to confuse the two types of measurements, especially when compensating a supplier. For example, it makes little sense to grant an extra reward to a supplier based on its ability to perform against *maintenance* measurements, since the company is paying out a reward in exchange for no material improvement in its condition.

The exact set of measurements selected for each supplier will vary by industry, company, and function, so we only make general recommendations here. Maintenance measurements should focus on transaction error rates and processing times, such as the number of rooms not cleaned by the janitorial staff, or the number of accounts payable billings that were paid early. Performance measurements should focus on anything that a company considers to be value-added, such as cost savings, increased revenue generation, added customers, or other measurable activities that can be clearly traced to an increase in profitability. For example, all early payment discounts can be taken, the cost per unit produced can be reduced, or the distribution cost per mile of freight delivery can be dropped. These are examples of "hard" measurements that result in clear profitability improvements, not measures that do not have a clear impact, such as answering customer complaint calls two seconds faster than was previously the case. Again, a company must create these measurements based on its own circumstances—no two companies will measure their outsourcing suppliers in exactly the same way.

Once the management team has derived an acceptable set of measurements, it must measure current operations with them, so that it has a baseline operations standard against which it can measure the performance of the supplier. By creating this baseline, it also gives the supplier little room to complain that the standards against which it is operating are too high—after all, the company attained those standards itself prior to handing over operations to the supplier.

Finally, the company should measure supplier performance at fixed intervals, using the exact same calculations every time. By doing so, period-to-period measurements are highly comparable. If there is any valid reason for altering the method by which a measurement is calculated, then the new method should be used to recalculate all previous measurements, since this creates a comparable set of measurements over a long time line.

These steps—creating measurements, establishing a baseline, and measuring performance at regular intervals—are an excellent way to establish control over a supplier's outsourcing operations.

Pros and Cons of Outsourcing Various Functional Areas

In this section, we cover the advantages and disadvantages of outsourcing nearly all corporate functions, from accounting to sales. This will be of assistance to those companies that are uncertain of how they can use outsourcing, and require a quick overview of how it may be used.

The outsourcing of the accounting function may be subdivided into a number of smaller categories. The most commonly outsourced tasks are the processing of payroll and tax forms, since they require particular skills that may not be present in smaller companies. Collections can also be shifted to a supplier, which brings a great deal of collection energy to the task, but runs the risk of irritating customers, and can be very expensive (one-third of the amount collected is the typical fee). Most local auditing firms would be happy to provide internal auditing services, which has the advantages of great expertise and minimal personnel training requirements, but usually at a vastly higher cost than can be attained internally. A few suppliers, such as Andersen Consulting, are also providing transaction processing services for accounts payable and billings. This option can be expensive, but also frees the controller from becoming bogged down in a relatively mundane task. The outsourcing of more complex tasks, such as financial analysis and cost accounting, is generally not recommended, since this requires great skill and familiarity with corporate information systems that cannot be quickly learned by outsiders. It may also reveal confidential information about company finances that management may not want in the hands of a supplier. Thus, payroll and taxation are the most commonly outsourced tasks in the accounting function, with lesser attention being paid to other areas.

There are many tasks within the general category of computer services that are well worth the effort to outsource, while others are generally maintained by in-house personnel. Nearly all companies, even those with large and experienced computer staffs, will occasionally require the services of outside "gurus" to repair seemingly intractable problems with their hardware or software. This is the most minimal form of outsourcing, though it is quite expensive on a per-hour basis. It is also possible to outsource data center management, which is particularly enticing, due to the capital investment in computer equipment that is no longer required. Also, if the supplier already runs the company's packaged software in its data center, then it may be able to reduce the number of software licenses leased from the software provider, though this is understandably frowned upon by software providers (who lose revenue when this happens). Because of the efficiencies associated with operating a large data center, this is also one of the few cases in which a company may be able to reduce its costs by outsourcing. Another good use for outsourcing suppliers occurs when a company has an adequate staff for maintaining the current computer systems, but has no internal capability for switching to a new system. In this case, the current staff continues to maintain the old system, while the supplier's staff installs a new one, and then either commences to manage it or trains the existing staff in the new system, and then withdraws from anything but a supporting role. Finally, there is the option of using an off-site help center, which has the advantage of using a centralized database of problems and resolutions but is much more expensive than an in-house staff if it includes an on-site repair team. Due to the wide array of available outsourcing solutions, this is an area in which it may make sense to use different suppliers for different functions, which the management team can manage either separately or through a designated lead supplier, who will provide (and charge for) additional management expertise in this role.

The customer service function can be outsourced if the supplier can be linked to the company through an online database that allows people in an off-site call center to enter customer orders and complaints into the system, as well as to review order status information. If so, there are a number of excellent telemarketing firms specializing in in-bound customer calls that can take over this function in its entirety. The cost tends to be equivalent to the in-house cost, since call center suppliers operate very large facilities that deal with so much call volume that their cost per call is quite low. They are also managed by personnel who are deeply experienced in the customer service function, and who can customize the customer contact experience so much that customers will never know they are talking to the employee of a supplier, and not the company. In addition, some call center operators, such as SITEL (based on Omaha, Nebraska), specialize in creating and managing new call centers on extremely short notice (it has been done in as little as 90 days), which can be a great boon to those companies who are rapidly rolling out new products, and who anticipate a great deal of customer service support on short notice. Outsourcing customer service can also extend to the use of a field service supplier, which keeps a company out of the business of managing a large staff of employees who are positioned in outlying locations. However, outsourcing customer service only works if there is a great deal of call volume, since suppliers are not interested in incurring the overhead cost associated with low-volume customer service functions. Also, it will not work if the company's database cannot be linked to the call center, since there is no other effective way to deal with customer inquiries and orders. Finally, many call centers specialize in only certain industries, such as magazine subscriptions or package delivery, and so may not be willing to enter a new industry. In short, this is a good alternative for larger companies with large customer service departments, but only for selected industries.

The engineering function can be outsourced if a company has only a part-time need for engineers, if the department is poorly managed, or if the quality of in-house engineers is low. In all these cases, we can assume that management is faced with an engineering staff that is so small or inadequate that it is forced to find help elsewhere. However, most companies who do not suffer from these engineering problems will *not* opt for outsourcing, because the engineering function may be the company's "core competency," which would put too much control over the company's future in the hands of a supplier. Also, the cost of outsourced engineering services is usually quite high, while there is also a risk that the supplier may spread company confidential information to competitors, despite the presence of a confidentiality agreement. For all these negative reasons, only those companies with a poor or small internal engineering capability will be interested in outsourcing their engineering departments.

There are many components to the human resources function, such as benefits administration, recruiting, outplacement, and training. Some of these functions can be outsourced, whereas others are best kept in-house. Recruiting is frequently shifted to outside recruiting firms, though this is a very expensive option that can be partially mitigated by putting the recruiting suppliers on retainer. Employee training can be shifted to a supplier in the majority of situations, since the bulk of training classes cover standardized topics that are easily updated by suppliers, and taught by practiced instructors. However, there are also company-specific classes on highly specialized topics that require at least an in-house writing staff to create the classes, as well as trainers for these topics. Outsourcing services, such as counseling and job placement assistance, is the most commonly outsourced task within the human resources field. Most companies do not lay off a sufficiently large number of employees to require the services of full-time outplacement and counseling professionals, and so the outsourcing decision is an easy one. Finally, benefits administration can be outsourced, but this involves the clerical handling of paperwork that is almost always least expensive when retained in-house. Given the large number of different areas in which outsourcing can be used, there is an additional problem of having to oversee the activities of a number of different suppliers, which may require the services of an extra in-house manager.

The single most commonly outsourced function is janitorial services, though its attendant function of maintenance services is outsourced considerably less frequently. The difference between the two is that janitorial services requires a minimal level of manual skill, which most companies prefer to have a supplier handle, whereas maintenance (frequently of highly specialized equipment) requires the services of talented and well-trained individuals that companies must go out of their way to retain. The primary instance in which the outsourcing of maintenance is a good idea is for the maintenance of HVAC (heat, ventilation, and air conditioning), because this involves the maintenance of equipment that is concentrated in just a few brands and the operation of which is well known.

An increasingly important outsourcing area is manufacturing. Companies can experience a reduction in costs and an increase in product quality by shifting their production to a supplier who is more knowledgeable in manufacturing best practices, uses better equipment, has a lower labor cost structure, or has greater efficiencies of scale. This approach also keeps management from becoming mired in the oversight of the production department, as well as avoid a large capital investment in plant and facilities. In addition, there is no risk of attracting the attention of manufacturing-oriented labor unions. A variation on the situation is to manufacture product components in-house, but to contract with distributors to conduct final assembly at their distribution warehouses, which has the signal advantage of allowing customers to order from a wide range of product features, while forcing the company to build products only up to the stage of production prior to where all the extra features are added, which reduces the number of inventory items to keep in stock. The primary disadvantages of using a manufacturing supplier are that it may have a poor delivery record or product quality; both of these factors can be reduced by a careful review of the references of potential suppliers, as well as operational reviews, prior to selecting one. Of course, those companies that already consider themselves to have attained a world-class competency in the manufacturing area will have no need to resort to outsourcing.

Logistics outsourcing is one of the most rapidly expanding fields in outsourcing, involving the freight, warehousing, freight brokerage, and freight auditing subfunctions. Only the largest companies can afford to efficiently operate their own trucking fleets, which would otherwise sit idle for some time period. To avoid this, they can outsource their freight operations to dedicated freight companies, which have greater economies of scale and much higher levels of efficiency. Also, several freight brokerage firms are now entering the business of storing and shipping a company's finished goods as needed, which carries with it the advantage of a reduction in fixed warehousing costs, as well as expert assistance in determining the least expensive ways to transport goods. Finally, outsourced freight auditing has long been a good way to ensure that freight is billed correctly from freight carriers; these firms charge for their services only if they find and collect on freight savings, so it has no attendant cost if a company was not already conducting an in-house auditing function. However, the suppliers of the most advanced warehousing and freight brokerage functions are interested only in large outsourcing deals, because there is a large start-up and continuing overhead cost when a supplier takes on a new customer. Consequently, smaller companies are able to outsource only their freight and freight auditing functions.

Within the sales and marketing department, one can outsource the advertising, sales, publicity, and telemarketing functions. In the advertising and publicity areas, outsourcing is especially appealing when there is not enough in-house work to require the services of a full-time person, and also because advertising and publicity firms are stocked with enough talent to yield better results. The downside to this approach is that advertising and publicity suppliers charge much more per hour than a company will pay to its in-house staff. Sales can also be shifted to independent distributors or salespeople, who are paid only if they can sell product, which reduces fixed sales costs. However, these sales personnel may be selling competing products at the same time, so this can be an unreliable sales method. In addition, an independent salesperson charges a high commission, so the variable sales cost is high. Finally, telemarketing firms will solicit orders through their outbound call centers on behalf of a company. This is a good approach if a company does not have an efficient in-house telemarketing function, or if it needs to rapidly develop the capability and cannot do so in-house. However, telemarketing suppliers are mostly interested in call volumes in the thousands per day and will charge a premium for call volumes lower than that level. Consequently, the cost of outside services is a key factor in sales outsourcing, as well as a loss of control over the sales staff.

The final area in which outsourcing can be applied is administration. This is a catchall function that includes such tasks as copying, temporary clerical services, record storage, security, and office management. Copy centers are widely available for the outsourcing of a company's copying needs and will even create an in-house copy center that they operate. This eliminates the cost and trouble of buying and maintaining expensive copying equipment but is more expensive on a per-sheet basis. Temporary clerical services will recruit temporary office staff on behalf of a company, which is especially useful for smaller companies that do not want a full-time recruiting person to handle this function; however, the supplier will charge a stiff hourly premium for the services of its temporary employees. Record storage centers will pick up and store a company's older records, as well as retrieve and return those that are needed. However, there is a time delay in the retrieval process. There are a multitude of security firms that are willing to recruit and train security personnel to guard company facilities, which is an area that many companies do not wish to handle for themselves. The main deterrent here is the markup in hourly fees that the suppliers take as their profit. Finally, very small firms can rent space from suppliers that provide a central office area that services a number of companies, including the services of an office manager and receptionist. This is an excellent approach for very small companies that do not have the resources or need for a full-time staff, though it is impractical once a company reaches a sufficient size to warrant hiring its own staff.

The main factors that arise out of this brief overview of outsourcing the various company functions are that there are many subfunctions within each department that can be selectively outsourced and that a company's particular circumstances will drive the need to outsource. This option is not for all companies, but it can be exceedingly useful in specific situations, and so requires a careful analysis of the situation before being used.

Summary

In this chapter, we have reviewed the steps that a management team should use to ensure that it is selecting the right supplier, negotiates a favorable contract, and continues to manage and measure the supplier in such a manner as to ensure that the outsourced function produces results that meet corporate expectations. However, the management team must be very clear about *why* it is engaging in outsourcing, or else its expectations will be very difficult to meet. Consequently, a great deal of up-front thought must be given to the reasoning behind the outsourcing decision prior to contracting with a supplier.

Evaluating the Operations of the Business

Chapter **7**

Professional Advisors

A s noted at the outset of this book, all businesses need to plan; businesses that plan well are businesses that take maximum advantage of opportunities. But making a successful go of any enterprise is a continuing process demanding expertise in many disciplines. The creative genius who started the business may not be skilled in negotiating with labor or with material suppliers; he or she may not be an expert on the tax consequences of decisions or on legal obligations.

Typically, businesses of all sizes use people from outside the business to advise management. The ways in which these advisors are selected are as varied as the businesses themselves. These methods vary from formal requests for proposals (RFPs) for consulting services, to a phone call to one's lawyer or accountant that begins "I've got a quick question for you ..." and ends some more than short time later with a free answer. Sometimes the expression "You get what you pay for" applies to free advice.

Small businesses often lack the in-house capability to perform the analysis and research associated with the more difficult business decisions. Individual or informal advice may not adequately address a problem that has consequences across the board. The best-qualified advice may come from a team of advisors, each knowledgeable in his field, and each with a knowledge of the business. The problem facing small businesses is assembling such a team. Often, consulting and advisory businesses will not have the necessary mix of disciplines within their organization. Few accounting firms or engineering firms have lawyers as part of their normal business operation. Their objective should be to recruit and manage a well-rounded team of advisors.

The first step in assembling an advisory team is to determine the business's "strength on the bench"—which disciplines are represented by qualified individuals on the staff. These individuals may or may not be used in the team. One may want fresh ideas from outside the business, preferring to use in-house staff as reviewing or critiquing authority.

However, participation by in-house staff with the team can be very valuable in ensuring that the team is considering the proper components of the business and is working toward the appropriate objectives. In-house expertise often can address information problems of the team and more cheaply provide the missing information. Also, in-house staff can be very effective as an information source in helping to identify internal problems.

Building a Team of Advisors

In striving for expertise in all areas related to the business, it makes sense for advisors to work with and for the business as a team. Even though there may be some overlapping of expertise in specific areas, such overlap may lead to healthy, differing opinions.

The following areas of expertise should be considered:

Law

In proper long- and short-term planning, many major (and minor) considerations will have legal consequences.

- *Organizational form.* Each form—a sole proprietorship, partnership, subchapter S corporation, limited partnership, or any other of a large number of business forms—has legal advantages and disadvantages. The consequences should be explored before one commences operation.
- *Contracts.* Contracts can have significant implications in both the sale and acquisition of products, materials, and services. The terms

can commit a business to long-term arrangements affecting significant portions of its resources.

- *Patents.* Everything from how to obtain a patent to the purchase, sale, and leasing of patent rights can be complex legal transactions of a very specialized nature. Few generalist lawyers have ever dealt with the U.S. Patent Office. Still fewer are licensed patent lawyers. Many "patent attorneys" cannot otherwise practice law.
- *Copyrights.* The practice of copyright law is another specialized field of the legal profession, subject to special rules and procedures.
- *Leases.* Like contracts, leases are often long-term commitments of resources that may have significant consequences even after the business may have ceased to exist. For example, a retail store or restaurant may have to execute a three-year lease with rent increases and renewal provisions. If after two years the store has the opportunity to move to a better location the lease may not permit the store to move. Or, at least, it will still have to pay for the first location. The lease may have binding consequences.
- *Zoning.* Where one wishes to locate or to expand or if one wants to change the nature of the business may be prohibited or restricted by existing zoning requirements. Zoning can be changed or variances obtained by petition to and approval of a zoning board.
- *Labor agreements.* Labor agreements are contracts between management and labor for the provision of a service in exchange for a price. Labor agreements are very specialized contracts governed by substantial federal labor law. Labor law practice is itself a highly specialized area of the law.
- *Warranties.* Warranties are typically assurances about the product or services. Warranties can be expressed in the terms and conditions of sales, but more often there are implied warranties. The Pinto automobile is a case involving an implied warranty of fitness and safety. In essence, the claim is that Ford produced a car that was unsafe for transporting human beings. It therefore violated an implied warranty. Implied warranties arise as a result of a business holding itself out as a provider of a product or service.
- *Lawsuits.* It was once said that "When the first lawyer moved to town, he nearly starved to death. When the second lawyer moved

in, they both got rich." Lawsuits can be both offensive and defensive. They can be very effective at forcing action or mandating inaction.

Banking

We have discussed at length the necessity of establishing a sound working relationship with a banker. By working with a banker and understanding the bank's needs and requirements, one may be able to forewarn the bank of some anticipated changes in status. An association with the bank will also give one financial advice that may extend beyond the in-house abilities of the bank itself. For example, selling stock or bond issues may be arranged through a bank with a broker.

Insurance

Insurance might be nothing more than order taking or claims processing, but it may be more. Insurance can constitute risk management and financing for the business. Some of the areas to consider include:

- *General liability.* This is a policy intended to compensate for losses associated with the general operations of the business.
- *Product liability.* Here, a company is insuring against damages occurring to persons and property by defects in the product. The famous case in this area is the exploding pop bottle case. There, a person was severely cut when a bottle of pop, which presumably had been overly carbonated, exploded. The asbestos and Pinto cases are similar examples. The real problems are the risk and extent of liability. Most insurance policies have limits on the recoveries allowed. Often, the judgments exceed those limits. The cost of liability insurance is directly related to the amount of coverage and inversely related to the deductible. One must seriously consider this trade-off.
- *Casualty.* Insurance can be purchased to protect against large losses generally due to disaster (fire, hurricanes, high winds, hail, etc.). As with all insurance, one must balance the risk of loss against the cost of protecting against that loss.

- *Life and health insurance.* The size of the business affects the type and nature of the insurance. If the business is owned by a few principals who are the chief operating personnel of the business, then the loss of one member could have serious consequences. As the business grows larger, providing employee life and health insurance becomes an employee benefit, which may become part of a package offered to induce hiring. It may also be necessary for negotiations with union representatives. Often, employee life insurance can be a valuable source of low-cost financing for the business. If a company insures its employees with a policy carrying a cash surrender value, and offers it as a benefit to the employee as a term policy, then the company may be able to borrow against that policy.
- *Pensions.* A company may set up self-insurance or purchase policies that will pay an annuity at some later date to retiring employees.
- *Loss of business and credit insurance.* A company may wish to protect against unusual bad debt losses in extending trade credit. Credit insurance is available, although not to cover against losses normally incurred in the industry. These losses, sometimes called primary losses, are distinct for each industry. Insurance is usually restricted to certain acceptable risks, as determined, for example, by a Dun & Bradstreet rating. The cost of this form of insurance varies directly with the risk of the accounts accepted and is calculated as a percentage of sales. The decision to purchase credit insurance depends on the probability of large credit losses, the company's ability as a self-insurer to bear those losses, and the cost of the premiums.

Marketing

This is an area in which a company's participation may be market directed. If it sells a highly visible consumer product (soft drinks, jeans, breakfast cereal, etc.), the services of advertising and marketing consultants usually becomes significant. As the products enter the secondary markets (chemicals, extrusions, fasteners, etc.), the need for marketing changes. New consultants and advisors can be used. The nature of the function changes significantly, and so may the magnitude of the expenditures. Advertising may be restricted to trade publications and catalogs. As a result, a marketing consultant may be a substantial and necessary component within the team concept.

Accounting

With the complexity of today's businesses, the answer to the simple question "How much did it cost to make?" results in the simple answer "It depends." Actually, that is an accurate answer because it does depend on how one looks at costs and revenues. The costs for regulation, taxes, and operations may well all be different. The reasons are varied and complex. For example, a machine used by a regulated entity may have to be depreciated on a straight-line basis for regulatory accounting purposes. For tax purposes, the firm will probably take the fastest depreciation permitted under the tax code. For operations, depreciation may have no relationship to time because it may simply be a function of use or of technology changes.

Because of the sheer complexity of our economy, the rapidly changing regulatory and tax environment, and the speed of technological obsolescence, one may have to call upon expert accounting assistance to meet these challenges.

Others

From time to time, it may be extremely useful to consult with other people such as:

- *Customers.* Often, the best source of information concerning product quality, perception in the market, price, advertising, and the like may be customer surveys, questionnaires, and interviews.
- *Former customers.* Owners of your product who have switched to competitors' products can sometimes provide valuable information on market perception and buying habits.
- *Suppliers.* Suppliers can give valuable insight into procurement costs and problems that may have future pricing consequences. They may also have ideas for substitute products or materials. Finally, suppliers may have knowledge concerning the needs and requirements of competitors.

- *Engineers.* Engineers can provide help ranging from minor engineering changes to entire operating plans. For example, engineers can be consulted on something as simple as finding a cheaper fastener for joining two components together, whereas a mining engineer may be called on to help design a 20-year mining plan. In some cases, governmental regulations may require the filing of engineering plans prior to the commencement of operations.

Selecting Individuals

Having determined the type and number of disciplines that need to be represented on the team, the next question is whom to select and how to select them. Some of the criteria include:

- *Level of experience.* The level of experience is probably the most important criterion. There simply is no substitute for experience. Here, the old adage applies: "It is good to profit from your own experience, but it is better to profit from the experience of others." Very often, consultants with experience in solving the problems of others may efficiently help to solve yours.
- *Secondary areas (overlap of expertise).* Often, an individual with various specialties (e.g., law, engineering, and business) may be able to fashion solutions creatively using a multidisciplinary approach. For example, an accountant-lawyer may be able to write a contract with creative delivery and payment clauses that will have a favorable tax effect.
- *Availability.* When considering hiring a consultant or getting an advisor, be sure that you get what you pay for. One may hire a lawyer only to find that on the day of an important hearing, he or she has a conflict and sends a partner who knows little about the case or, worse, an associate who knows nothing.

  Sometimes the consultant may have other business commitments with greater financial rewards and your project has to wait. One way to avoid this is to schedule and confirm in advance. Also, be explicit in your expectations. Make sure they can't say, "We didn't know that was what you expected."

- *Cost.* Cost is listed fourth but it is usually the first or second in importance. Generally, try to get the best advice within a budget. Commonly referred to as "bang for the buck," this figure is negotiable but you must ensure that you are getting what you want and paying what you expected to pay to get it.

  A good contract lawyer can be of assistance. For example, a percentage of final payment may be withheld to assure that the product or service meets specifications and needs. Often, contracts will permit draws based on satisfactory completion of identifiable milestones. Sometimes guarantees and warranties are conditions of payment.

  Another consideration of cost is the competitive price offered for services. There is no harm in asking, "What is it going to cost? What can I expect to pay? How will I be billed? Who will work on the project and what rate do they bill at?" Ask for a breakdown of the estimated cost of the project by task, by individual. Question contingencies and miscellaneous costs.

- *Conflicts of interest.* Establish a conflict of interest policy. Once the policy is established, it should be written, discussed, and distributed to all vendors of services seeking to work for you. Conflicts of interest can be especially difficult to assess because the experience of others is what one is seeking from an advisor. If that advisor has worked for a competitor, his advice may be doubly valuable. But remember, if they talk *to* you, they may talk *about* you, and others may profit from information about you. Evaluate what they tell you about others. Is it the kind of information you want others to know about you? It might be valuable to expect from the advisor a commitment to nondisclosure of trade or confidential information. Most advisors have no problem with this.

- *Concordance with your advisors.* You should be able to develop a good working relationship with your advisors and feel mutual respect. An advisor is an advisor—he does not run the business, nor is he responsible for making a success of it. The best advisors are those who work themselves out of a job. You should strive for self-sufficiency, resorting to experts only for extraordinary situations.

Hire advisors who expect to help the business on an "as needed" basis but are willing to keep in touch or stay current on your status. This can be encouraged through fee arrangements called retainers.

Organization and Structure

How the advisory team fits into the organizational structure can be answered in many ways. Some businesses have adopted the team as part of the staff function of the firm, giving it official status and requiring it to comply with the company's structural rules. Others treat advisory teams in an informal manner. Some of the advantages to an informal association of advisors include:

- *Greater independence of thought and operation.* When an advisory body becomes institutionalized, it loses some of its autonomy. That is not to say that the advisory group should not have definite lines of reporting, accountability, and responsibility. It simply means that it may not be bound by rigid structural constraints.
- *By being an informal functioning entity, without line authority, it is clear that advisors are advisors and not decision makers.*
- *More freedom of action.* Informal organizational structures permit the team to cross different lines of authority. This permits better problem solving. Often, problems cross lines of authority and are systematic rather than isolated.
- *Fewer controls.* Most advisory team functions should not be bound by notice of meeting, elections, and minutes requirements. These, although needed in a structured organization, are often a burden to problem solving. Unstructured, free thinking may lead to quicker solutions to problems.
- *Planning versus review.* Advisory teams are generally more beneficial when used for planning rather than only review. Planning is less reactive to existing or past conditions, and as such must be responsive to environmental changes. If advisors are put in a review mode, then a more structured formal approach is better. For planning, the team must be responsive to unplanned opportunities as they arise.

- *Compensation.* Although late in the list, compensation should be anticipated, considered, and discussed early in the process. Agreement should be reached on a workable approach for paying advisors. It should be remembered that not all advice is rendered at meetings and that preparation is necessary to delivering most good advice. Generally, fixed retainers are used to compensate for those unstructured work requirements, but other methods may be devised.
- *Uniformity of compensation.* Different advisors are paid differently. Pay is a function of individual contracts and services. Several advisors may work in a team, but uniformity of pay is not automatic.

The goal is to get what you pay for. You are hiring advisors because of their skill and independent thinking. They should not be tied to thinking of how things have been done in the past. It may be just such thinking that has gotten the firm into whatever dilemma it now faces. An objective review of the current status may be necessary, but advisors should not be restricted to thinking, "That's the way we've always done it."

Working Together

Assembling a multidisciplinary group of advisors may cause as many problems as it solves. Consider the following sources of possible trouble:

- *Differing work styles.* An awareness of how other people work is usually helpful in getting things done. For example, an individual who is concerned with detail should be able to work and respect a creative individual who focuses more on the big picture. There is, however, a big gap between "should" and "do." Therefore, have explicit expectations and discussions concerning work styles and what is expected of each member. Often, a facilitator has a place on the team to ensure a unified attitude among the participants. This person, regardless of expertise or discipline, can apply the synergy to the various parts and personalities on the team.

- *Turf problems.* From any professional's viewpoint, there are overlapping areas of expertise. For example, lawyers and accountants may both have significant tax experience. Coming from differing perspectives can cause problems, but it may also create opportunities. You may not want unity of thought from your advisors but you certainly do not want open warfare. One method of avoiding or minimizing open hostilities and turf battles is to obtain a list from the potential advisors of individuals (of other disciplines) whom they have worked with in the past. Also, confidential conversations and interviews with the consultants will bring out areas of possible difficulties in working relationships.

- *Attitudes toward risk.* Some individuals are more averse to risk than others. Because the object of using advisors is to get advice, and not to take risks, this should be a minimal problem. However, the concern is that the advisors should be pulling in the same direction. One of the objectives of the advisory team is to consider the risk effects of the solutions. The decision concerning the minimal acceptable risk is management's decision; whether the advisors agree on the risk effect should be of some concern to you.

- *Time availability.* Because advisors are not full-time employees, their time is not necessarily yours. Competing interests occupy the advisors' time; advisors are interested in selling their time and may have scheduling problems in meeting your needs. Here is where a coordinator is essential. Pulling the team together may at times be very time consuming and tax patience. Request availability schedules when recruiting and interviewing. But be aware that most schedules are subject to change.

Summary

Asking for and getting the right advice is a learned skill. From the start, you need to evaluate your in-house skills, strengths, and weaknesses, and should seek advice for those weaknesses. You may wish to test the quality of your strengths by working with advisors in those areas. The selection process for advisors can be more difficult than selecting employees. The evaluation of their skills may come too late in the process to seek better advisors.

As with hiring employees, advisors bring their own prejudices and opinions as to how things should be done. They may be hard to work with or they may not have the same risk and business philosophy as your management. But as with any business decision, the risks of a bad decision can be minimized through assimilation of data, analysis of qualifications, checking with references and former clients, and examination of credentials. Finally, you should be willing to commit the resources necessary to see the project through—although you should also be ready to bail out in the event that the advisor is ineffective.

Chapter 8

Business Valuation

There comes a point in the life of almost every small business when, for a variety of reasons, the owner is interested in placing a value on that business. This chapter will present an overview of the reasons for valuation and methods of obtaining it for small businesses.

Reasons for Valuation

Certainly, if one is making a determination to sell a portion or all of a business, it is important to have an idea of the value of that business. It is also important to recognize that the sale of a partial interest of a business may not be a pro rata share of the value of the whole. For example, a minority interest of 40 percent may not be as valuable to a potential buyer on a proportionate basis as a controlling interest of 51 percent.

Even if the business is not going to be sold, there may be other "quasi-sales" reasons for putting a value on the business. For example, one may wish to establish employee stock option plans, whereby over time the employees become shareholders in the business. Such an employee stock option plan (ESOP) requires an annual valuation of the business in order to establish a value for the shares placed into the ESOP for the employees.

Another reason for a valuation is anticipation of "going public"—positioning to sell stock in a public market. Valuation will tell the approximate value per share to be expected from the market for the stock.

Other reasons for placing a value on the business have to do with estate planning by the owners of the business. In order to make a determination of the size of gifts that owners may wish to make in various years, it is important to have an annual evaluation of the gifts as they are made. One may wish to have a valuation made in order to determine the gift taxes to be paid or the best ways to save on those gift and estate taxes. The valuation may also be used to determine a way of recapitalizing the stock in order to let the current owner(s) retain control of the business, while passing the value of the business, or its appreciation in value, into the estate. One may want a value in anticipation of the purchase of life insurance to be used to provide for continuity of the business in the event of the death of a key individual. Life insurance is often used to cover an agreed-upon buy–sell arrangement among owners in the business, in the event of the death of one of the principals. Through a regular valuation process, one has current values to use among the owners as well as with tax people.

Valuation is necessary when a company has the opportunity or the desire to spin off a part of the business into a separate legal entity or when it is acquiring or merging with another legal entity. Condemnations also require valuation to make a determination of business damages associated with the taking of property by a governmental entity. The legal reorganization of the business, either through bankruptcy or other proceedings, may require a formal valuation. Finally, two of the more unpleasant reasons for valuation have to do with ownership disputes. Sometimes these disputes among partners lead to dissolution of that partnership. Divorce, where the business is a part of the estate of the couple and that estate has to be divided between the divorced parties, also requires valuation.

Valuation Methods and Theories

Without a doubt, the single most influential publication in the area of business valuation is Internal Revenue Service Ruling 59–60. Although the revenue ruling was written specifically for estate and gift tax purposes, the concepts applied in the ruling have been generally held to be of use in any valuation for business purposes.

Section Three, .01 states:

A determination of fair market value, being a question of fact, will depend upon the circumstances in each case. No formula can be devised that will be generally applicable to the multitude of different valuation issues arising in estate and gift tax cases. Often, an appraiser will find wide variances of opinion as to the fair market value of a particular stock. In resolving such differences, he should maintain a reasonable attitude in recognition of the fact that valuation is not an exact science. A sound valuation will be based upon all the relevant facts, but the elements of common sense, informed judgment and reasonableness must enter into the process of weighing these facts and determining their aggregate significance.

One might note that the paragraph is directed toward estate and gift tax cases but its strictures can be and have been more widely applied. The processes described in the revenue ruling are applicable to sole proprietorships and partnerships as well as corporations. In fact, later rulings gave broad, general application to these concepts.

Section Three, .03 states: "Valuation of securities is, in essence, a prophecy as to the future and must be based on facts available at the required date of appraisal." "Prophecy as to the future" refers to the concept of future value, which is dependent on income potential.

Section Four lists eight separate factors that should be considered in any valuation process. While these factors may not be all-inclusive, they are essential and should be considered whenever a valuation is being performed.

1. *The nature of the business and the history of the enterprise since its inception.* The history will show the entity's stability or lack of stability, its growth or lack of growth, and its diversity or lack of diversity. The amount of detail that should be considered will increase as the date of appraisal approaches. Recent events are of greater help in predicting the future than events in the past. The financial results of the business events of the past that are unlikely to recur in the future should be discounted, because value is most closely related to future expectancies.

2. *The economic outlook in general and the conditioned outlook of the specific industry in particular.* Every business fits into the general economy and must be looked at with consideration of where the economy appears to be going. However, some businesses do not respond in direct relationship to the economy in general. Therefore, it is very important to look at the economic impacts on the specific industry as well.

3. *The stock and the financial condition of the business.* If available, balance sheets should be obtained in comparative format for a period of two or more years. Balance sheets as of the date of the appraisal, or at the most recent possible date, would also be helpful. From the balance sheets, the appraiser should be able to determine such things as the liquidity status, the book value of fixed assets, working capital, solvency, and net worth.

4. *The earning capacity of the company.* If available, income statements should be obtained in comparative format for a period of five years. Such income statements should show gross income as well as principal deductions by major product lines. Particular emphasis may be placed on salaries of owners or officers of the business. In addition, income available for dividends and dividends actually paid will be of particular interest, as will increases in retained earning and adjustments necessary to balance retained earning against the balance sheet: "Prior earnings records usually are the most reliable guide as to the future expectancy. Resorting to arbitrary 5- or 10-year averages without regard to current trends or future prospects will not produce a realistic valuation."

5. *Dividend paying capacity.* The primary emphasis in dividend paying capacity should be the ability to pay dividends rather than on dividends actually paid. It should be recognized that in many forms of businesses, dividends are avoided because of tax consequences. However, the ability to have paid dividends may be an important way to determine the value of the business.

6. *Whether the enterprise has goodwill or other tangible value.* Goodwill is, after all, a name for excess earning capacity. To determine *whether* a business has goodwill is difficult; to determine the *value* of goodwill is even more so. The value of goodwill rests on the ability of the business to earn a return greater than the industry's average return on its net assets.

7. *Sales of stock and the size of the block of stock to be valued.* If there have been sales of stock, those sales can be used to help determine the value of the business. If parts of the business have been valued, those interests may also be used to establish the value of the whole business. However, sales of an interest in closely held businesses, sole proprietorships, or partnerships are not always arm's-length transactions. Therefore, such sales must be considered carefully before being used to establish the value of the business as a whole. The concept of "blockage" has to do with minority interests. A minority interest may not always receive an estimate of value proportionate to the percentage of ownership that the block of stock represents.

8. *A market price of stocks in corporations engaged in the same or similar lines of business having their stock actively traded in open markets.* When it is possible to find comparable companies whose stock is traded on the open market, this information can be helpful in determining the value of the business. However, because the nature and size of the business are usually unique, it is very difficult to find truly comparable companies.

Methods of Obtaining Valuation

Now that we have discussed the reasons for valuation and the elements to be considered when obtaining one, it is time to look at the practical means of obtaining one.

Discounted Cash Flows

A strictly discounted cash flow method of valuation is future-oriented and is based on a limited-life projection. The method may be used effectively if it can be applied to limited-life income streams and situations such as:

- A project type of business that has a certain finish date.
- Contract term–oriented businesses.
- Situations in which early cash flow is the most important issue.
- Situations in which return on investment (payback) is the key concern.

FIGURE 8.1

Discounted Cash Flow Example

Year	Net Cash Flow	Discounting Factor at a 10% Rate	Present Value of Cash Flow
1	$1,250,000	.9009	$1,126,125
2	1,313,000	.8116	1,065,631
3	1,378,000	.7312	1,007,594
4	1,447,000	.6587	953,139
5	1,519,000	.5935	901,527
		Total	$5,054,016

The method may also be used if an approximation of a pro forma balance sheet can be made at some future date. The value of the residual assets are discounted as a part of the process.

An example of the discounted cash flow method is shown in Figure 8.1. In this example, we list estimated cash flows for the next five years and assume an increase in the flows from year-to-year of 5 percent, based on management judgments regarding the ability of the business to generate an increasing amount of cash based on either an increase in sales, a decline in expenses, or both. The positive annual cash flows are listed in the second column of the example. In the third column, we list a discounting factor. This discounting factor is used to reduce the value of future cash flows to a current cash amount. If this current cash amount were to be invested at a rate of return (as represented by the discount factor), it will earn interest income that, when added to the current cash amount, will equal the future cash flow amount from which it was originally discounted. Cash flows have a smaller present value if they will occur farther in the future, so the discounting factor becomes smaller for later periods, which results in a very small present value for a cash flow that is some distance in the future. In the example, cash flows are discounted by 10 percent for one year in the future, but by more than 40 percent for cash flows five years in the future. Because of the steep reduction in the value of cash flows that are far out in the future, a business valuation calculation that uses discounted cash flows will rarely include cash flows that are beyond the next 10 years—cash flows farther off in the future are so small as to be not worth adding to the calculation.

Given the considerable impact that the discounting factor has on a company's valuation, it is apparent that the reasoning behind the use of a particular discount rate is of paramount importance. This rate can be a firm's cost of capital, which is the blended cost of its debt and equity, or it can be the interest rate at which the company's investors can invest their funds elsewhere. Also, if the variability of future cash flows is volatile, then the discounting factor may be increased by several percentage points, which places a lower value on the company by reducing estimates of the present value of future cash flows.

Earnings Capitalization Approach

The earnings capitalization approach is intended to indicate what one would pay to receive a given amount of earnings. It is very similar to the method used for valuing an insurance annuity contract.

In order to use the method, (1) a "comparison" return for competing investments must be available, and (2) a risk differential must be considered.

The return considerations will include a basic "rent on money" as well as an inflation factor and a risk for the particular investment. To determine the basic rent on money, consider such things as: daily savings accounts, annual certificates of deposit, five-year Treasury notes, 20-year AAA corporate bonds, and the yield on blue-chip stocks.

First, determine the amount of return (in percentage) that the money should earn, then determine the amount of money the business will return. There are, of course, many ways to estimate that return. One can look at the income from a single year, the average of three to five years of history, a projection of the next several years, or a composite of any of the above.

Once the income from the business has been estimated and a necessary return has been established, the calculation is simply to divide the income by the necessary return expressed as a percentage. The resulting number is the value of the business.

The approach is fairly simple and does not resolve a number of problems such as how to adjust the income for certain tax and other considerations or the impact of negative earnings.

Adjustments to Income Statements

Before using any income statement numbers for valuation purposes, it is important to consider adjustments that may be necessary for those numbers to reflect accurately the value of the business. Among the items that need to be considered and adjusted for are:

- Excess compensation to the owners.
- Excess fringe benefits to the owners.
- Potential inventory value accumulations.
- Bad debt write-offs.
- Depreciation methodologies employed.
- Extraordinary write-offs.
- Synergistic economies
- Corporate income taxation.
- Investment tax credits.

Price/Earnings Multiple Method

The price/earnings method is often used to value publicly traded companies, and less so for closely held companies because:

- Such stock rarely has a ready market and, in fact, may be restricted.
- Reported earnings may have been significantly adjusted for tax purposes.
- The size of blocks of stock may differ widely.
- True comparables from a public area are hard to find. However, the price/earnings multiple method may be used as a good test of reasonableness of the capitalization rate method discussed earlier.

Adjusted Book Value Method

The adjusted book value method is an attempt to make a determination of the appraised value of the assets of the business. Typically, only those assets used in the operation of the business itself are used to make comparisons against competitors. Among the balance sheet items that will potentially require appraisal increments will be inventories, real estate, and equipment. Each asset of value is looked at independently, and an appraisal of the current value of that asset is made. Among the balance sheet adjustments that may be necessary in using this method are:

- Inventory.
- Bad debts.
- Fixed assets.
- Patents or franchises.
- Investments and affiliates.
- Goodwill and intangibles.
- Future royalties.
- Low-cost debt service.
- Tax loss carry-forwards.

Accounting Considerations

Both the income statement and the balance sheet may have been significantly affected by accounting policies employed by the business. Among the accounting policies that need to be considered and adjusted for are:

- Consolidated financial statements.
- Depreciation methods.
- Inventory accounting.
- Marketable securities.
- Accounts receivable.
- Amortization of intangibles.
- Research and development.
- Pension funds or profit sharing.
- Foreign exchange.
- Income tax deferrals.
- Deferred compensation.
- Installment sales.
- Overhead allocations.

Dividend-Paying Capacity Method

The dividend-paying capacity method mentioned in Internal Revenue Service Ruling 59–60 is an attempt to determine the dividends the company could have paid over some period of time, perhaps five years. It considers such factors as:

- The cash needs of the company for working capital.
- The cash needs of the company for expansion and growth.
- Contingencies and executory contracts.
- Debt.
- Salaries paid to owners.

Having considered these items and adjusted the dividend-paying capacity accordingly, you should determine an appropriate yield. The appraiser, in considering a yield, should consider comparable companies and the yield that could be realized from alternative investments. When the dividend-paying capacity in terms of dollars is known, and an appropriate yield in percentage terms has been given, divide the dividend-paying capacity by the yield expressed as a percentage, to arrive at an estimate of value.

Comparable Method

When the comparable method is used, one must be sure sales of the stock are from "comparable" companies. This means that they are truly comparable in terms of the nature of the business, the size of the business, the earnings of the business, and the size of the block of stock being traded.

If the business being valued has had recent purchase offers of its own stock, such values may be used—with appropriate cautions. Determine the changes that have occurred since that purchase offer and be aware of the amount of ownership involved. It is also important to look at the financial structuring of the offer to make sure that it, too, is comparable. Be sure the offer was a valid, arm's-length transaction.

It is important to consider recent sales to know for certain to whom the sale was made as well as any sweeteners or side deals that may have been involved.

Goodwill

There are many definitions of the concept of goodwill. Basically, goodwill is the ability of an entity to earn a higher-than-normal return on its investment in an asset. Among the ways that have been used for placing a value on goodwill are:

- The accountant's method.
- The profit opportunity method.
- The cost to create method.
- The cost savings method.
- The cost of purchase method.

The accountant's method is simply one of plugging a value in for goodwill after values have been assigned to all other assets. The amount of the goodwill is the amount of the purchase price which cannot be otherwise assigned to specific assets.

The profit opportunity method attaches a profit to a specific and tangible asset, such as a patent, and determines the present value of that profit over some period of time.

The cost to create method is similar to the construction cost method or the replacement cost method in real estate valuation. One must first identify all the costs that would be associated with creating the intangible asset. Often the intangible asset has no carrying value on the books and its cost to create will be in addition to what is shown on the books.

The cost savings method has to do with an asset that creates an opportunity for the business to save money because of the ownership of a process, patent, or the like. The methodology involves the present value of savings over some period of time.

Cost of purchase method is simply an estimate of what it would take if the firm went out into the market and bought a similar asset today.

Additional Valuation Methods for Acquisition Purposes

Thus far, we have discussed business valuation from the viewpoint of a company owner's business. The same valuation methods apply when determining the price a company is willing to pay for another business, plus a few additional methods. This section covers the extra methods.

In new or expanding markets, a competitor may invent a new product design that has considerable value by itself or will integrate nicely into a company's existing product line. If a company does not feel that it has the time to create a competing product, or if the competitor's product is too heavily defended by patents, the company should strongly consider purchasing the competitor, or at least the product or patents that it owns. Valuing this type of acquisition is extremely difficult, because the new product may have no proven cash flow on which to base a discounted cash flow analysis. Instead, the company must use one of two valuation methods. The first is to determine the cost the company would incur to develop and market a competing product, which should also include the cost of lost profits while the new product is being constructed. This method is based entirely on cost estimates. The second approach is to estimate the cash flows to be garnered if the competing product takes a reasonable portion of the market. The determination of estimates for this second method is also highly judgmental, and is based on not only market share estimates, but also estimates of price points and the extent of future competition. Of the two methods, the first is somewhat more accurate, since all estimates are based on internal costs, for which the engineering and marketing staffs should have some historical basis from previous product rollouts. Because the latter method contains so many variables, few of which are under company control, it can result in a wide range of possible valuations.

Despite the extremely imprecise nature of these estimating methods, companies in the high-technology sector regularly use them to purchase start-up companies that have developed new technology, even though there may be no sales history for the new products. In particular, Cisco Systems, Microsoft, and Yahoo! have been acquiring high-exclamation point technology and Internet companies at a prodigious rate in order to obtain new technologies. They are forced to value companies with these methods, because the time periods for the development of products is so short that they cannot hope to develop all possible technologies in-house, and so must acquire other companies to supplement their internal research and development efforts. However, these are *not* acceptable valuation methods for companies not locate din industries with a heavy reliance on new products or technology, because the methods can result in acquisition prices that are far removed from the actual cash flow results that the acquiring company is likely to obtain.

When calculating a purchase price for a potential acquisition candidate, the management team should not rely solely on the financial information presented by the acquiree. This is because the acquiree either is not aware of internal control problems that may be resulting in the improper reporting of financial information or it is using aggressive accounting methods or fraud to make its financial results look better than they really are. For these reasons, an acquiree's financial statements must be investigated further with a due diligence review.

The due diligence review can be a simple review of strictly financial matters, or one that includes significantly more detail, such as reviews of an acquiree's customer mix, the condition of its manufacturing equipment, or the remaining number of years left on its existing patents. This additional information may result in a significant change in the price that a company eventually offers an acquisition candidate, so it is best to conduct the full due diligence review, rather than one that just verifies the accuracy of the financial statements.

An example of the most common due diligence questions to be answered is noted in Figure 8.2. The list presented here is by no means complete, and should be supplemented by additional review questions that are tailored to the industry in which a company operates. For example, the review of an injection molding company would include a review of the condition of all company-owned molds. Alternatively, the review of a high-technology research company could exclude a fixed-asset review, since the only issue of significance to the acquiring company is the existence of patents and the applicability of the acquiree's ongoing research to the company's operations.

FIGURE 8.2

Sample List of Due Diligence Questions

Accounting and Finance

1. *Are operations matching budgeted performance levels?* If there are significant negative variances, review them to determine if they are one-time events or more indicative of continuing problems that will be a more permanent drag on earnings.

2. *Audit the fixed-asset list.* For some acquiring companies, the main reason for buying another company is to sell off some choice assets for an immediate return. Consequently, a detailed audit of all major assets becomes a key part of the due diligence process if there are many undervalued assets. It may also be necessary to have an appraisal done on the key assets, to ensure that they indeed have a significant resale value.

3. *Compare year-to-year financial statements for the last three years and investigate significant trends.* This step ensures that the acquiring company is fully aware of the reasons for any continuing increases in expenses or decreases in revenues that are likely to extend into the future and will therefore have an impact on the cash flow projections of the acquirer.

4. *Itemize all loans, as well as the stated interest rates, payoff terms, and covenants.* This information is necessary to determine the presence of unusually strict loan covenants that will insert the acquiree's lender into the daily operating decisions of the acquirer, not to mention unusually high interest rates that have high penalty payments for early payoffs.

5. *Obtain a copy of the budget.* This document may reveal drops or increases in revenue that the management team of the acquiree is anticipating but the acquiree has not yet experienced. Without this information, the due diligence review could uncover only variances that have already arisen.

6. *Obtain a detailed inventory list.* Use this list to review the inventory for both obsolescence and valuation. For the first item, visually check the inventory for evidence of age, such as old inventory count tags, shipping documentation, or anything else that contains a date. Also, if the acquiree's computer systems are sufficiently sophisticated, obtain a report from it that lists the inventory items by usage pattern or last date used, which reveals those items for which there are clearly surplus stocks on hand. For the second item, trace per-unit costs to supplier invoices for a sample of the inventory, to ensure that no costs have been artificially inflated. If some of the inventory is manufactured internally, then review the cost records for those items in terms of subsidiary-level parts, labor hours worked, and labor rates per hour.

7. *Obtain a list of all expenses included in overhead costs, as well as the detail of the overhead allocation formula.* Some companies will include expenses in the overhead category so that they can be allocated to inventory, rather than be expensed, which artificially improves profits. Also, the allocation methodology can likewise be altered to allocate too many expenses to inventory; for example, the

entire facility rent expense may be allocated to overhead, when in reality only that portion in which the production facility operates should be allocated.

8. *Obtain a list of all standard expense accruals.* See if any expenses are missing from this list that are typically accrued, such as vacation pay, salaries earned but not paid, and sales and income taxes payable. Including these extra accruals in the target company's financial statements may result in a significant reduction in the valuation of an acquiree.

9. *Obtain the most current credit report.* This is one of the easiest pieces of information to obtain about an acquiree, and includes all public records of liens on the assets of the acquiree. By comparing the liens list to the list of loans and leases provided by the acquiree, one can tell if any loans or leases are missing from the list provided by the acquiree.

10. *Review the accounts payable aging and review old, unpaid items.* If there is a significant proportion of old supplier invoices that are unpaid, there may be strained relations with key suppliers, as well as receiving problems that result in items not being correctly logged in to the inventory database (and therefore not paid, since there is no record of receipt).

11. *Review the accounts receivable aging for old, uncollected items and investigate.* Also look for invoices that have been credited and rebilled, because this will make them look newer. A large proportion of overdue accounts receivable not only represents a possible collection problem, but also possible product quality or shipping issues that customers are protesting by not paying.

12. *Verify any state or federal tax loss carryforwards.* These amounts can be substantial, and may even be the main reason for an acquisition. However, be sure to have a tax expert verify all prior tax returns in which losses occurred, as well as all current legislation regarding the use of the carryforwards, to ensure that the benefits being purchased can actually be used. Also, if the carryforward credits must be claimed over several future years, rather than all at once, be sure to discount the value of the credits over the years that will pass before they are entirely used up.

13. *Verify that the acquiree's lenders are willing to continue funding all existing debt.* A common contract clause for a lender to insert into a loan agreement is that the loan is immediately due and payable if there is a change of ownership in the borrower, so this clause must be waived, unless the acquirer has an alternate lending source that can finance the acquiree's debt.

14. *Verify the level of funding for such liabilities as pensions, litigation, or environmental remediation claims.* These can be significant amounts (especially the last one), and can sink an acquisition deal if the amounts are substantial.

15. *What depreciation schedule is used for major assets, and what salvage value is used as part of this calculation?* A company can increase the number of years over which its assets are depreciated, as well as increase their assumed salvage values, in order to reduce the overall depreciation expense. The acquiring company must then incur a greater expense when those assets are disposed of, because there will still be some unamortized depreciation on the books that must be expensed.

16. *What leases are current, and how long before they expire?* This issue is critical if the acquiring company wants to move the acquiree out of its current facilities for

centralization purposes, but must still pay the rent on the acquiree's facilities for some years into the future. This issue is of particular concern if the local economy is soft, because it is more difficult under those conditions to sublease the property. Alternatively, if one or more facility leases have unusually *inexpensive* terms and run for many more years, this can be an advantage for the acquiring company.

Competition

1. *What is the market share of major competitors?* If there is a trend toward some of these competitors and away from the acquiree over the last few years, this may be evidence of a serious decline in the acquiree's future business prospects. This analysis should focus only on those companies that compete directly against the acquiree in its specific market niches; information about other competitors is not relevant.

2. *What new products are competitors developing?* Some knowledge of new technology or product features that will soon be on the market will give a buyer some inkling of possible changes in the rate of sales growth for the products of an acquiree that will soon find itself competing against those new products, possibly calling for a change in projected sales levels for them. It may also be necessary to project reduced margins on those products, in case the best likely response to new product competition is a drop in price.

Computer Systems

1. *Determine the types and versions of all major software used in the target company.* This review will reveal whether the software systems already in place are so outmoded that additional expenses must be incurred to replace them. This cost should include the expense of transitioning data to the new software, as well as training employees in the use of the new system. If the software is adequate, but the version is an old one, then the buyer must also budget for extra funds to upgrade the software.

2. *Determine the adequacy of the computer network.* Have an expert networking consultant review the acquiree's network to see if it is a well-laid-out system with consistent wiring, high capacity (such as is provided by fiber-optic cabling), and is protected from electrical surges and power failures. Also, the network software should be of the most recent version, and one that is well supported both locally and by the network software company. If not, the buyer should budget for a replacement of the network hardware and/or software.

3. *Determine the age and capacity of all computers.* This information tells the buyer how many computers should be replaced in the near term, as well as the ability of the computers to store and use any new programs that the buyer may want to install in them.

Engineering

1. *What is the quality of the product design process and of the engineering staff?* A company that has a dominant design process and an excellent engineering staff that regularly churns out new products within its designated cost and time

budgets can be the largest single center of value for it and may have a profoundly positive impact on the valuation of the company. Alternatively, if the process results in continuing design iterations, flaws in released products, and time or cost overruns, the buyer may have to incur the considerable cost of replacing or overhauling the engineering function, as well as investing in a redesign of existing products that may be flawed.

2. *Does the engineering department use design software?* If not, the buyer may be able to greatly improve its design efficiency by installing computer-aided design software. Also, the buyer should see if the engineering staff uses a computerized design library that it can use to "cut and paste" predefined parts into new products, which greatly speeds the design process while also automatically creating a bill of materials.

3. *Determine the existence of and expiration dates on any patents owned by the acquiree.* This information tells the buyer when it can expect increased competition from other companies, as well as which product features are legally protected in the near term. Also, if the buyer is interested in suing other companies for suspected patent infringement, this information may be its primary reason for buying the company.

4. *Must the acquiree work around design patents held by competitors?* If the acquiree's products are clearly inferior to those of a competitor because it cannot use patented designs, the buyer must find out when those patents expire and determine if it can stand the lower level of market share until that time. In addition, the competitors who hold those patents may be able to extend them by filing for new patents that are based on incremental improvements to the old design; if so, the acquiree's products may be permanently in a secondary position to those of the competition, which will affect its ability to grow and earn a reasonable profit.

5. *What is the timeline for new product development?* If the acquiree has a potentially "hot" product line that will reach the market soon, then the buyer should alter its valuation upward to reflect the profitability of those new products, even though the margins from them can only be guessed, based on the sales of similar products in the same or a related market niche. The buyer should also be cognizant of the anticipated release dates of these new products, as well as their rollout costs, which should be factored into the anticipated cash flows it uses to derive the valuation of the acquiree.

6. *What is the sales and gross margin performance of new products?* The valuation of the acquiree will be higher if it has released new products that have a steep upward sales trend, as well as high gross margins. Alternatively, if the company's newest products do not have good prospects, then the buyer can reduce the valuation of the acquiree.

7. *What proportion of sales are from products that have been on the market for at least five years?* The buyer should know if the acquiree's products tend to die out quickly, or if it has a mix of steady performers that can be counted on to produce a steady sales pattern for a number of years to come. If the products tend to die out quickly, then the buyer should place considerable emphasis on the profitability

of all new products currently on the market, those that are soon to be released, and the quality of the product design process used by the acquiree.

Legal Issues

1. *Are there any current legal issues or a previous history of them?* The buyer needs to ascertain its maximum legal exposure from this information, so the search of legal records should go back at least five years and be as thorough as possible. Be particularly concerned with environmental lawsuits, since the monetary liability can be astronomically high. If the legal risk appears to be too great, but the buyer still wants to purchase the company, it should consider an asset purchase instead, which avoids legal complications.

2. *Obtain a list of all stockholders, with their proportions of ownership.* This tells the buyer whom it must contact regarding a purchase and which current owners are in a position to block the purchase. If necessary, the buyer may have to negotiate a private purchase of stock from selected owners, which will affect the total purchase price paid for the acquiree.

3. *Are there any environmental problems?* The buyer should conduct an environmental review of the acquiree's facilities, using an experienced engineering consultant to conduct the review. This should include groundwater tests to ensure that there are no potential dumping problems that the buyer will later have the responsibility for cleaning.

4. *Are there any current penalties not yet paid to the government for safety violations?* These reviews are conducted by the Occupational Safety and Health Administration (OSHA), which can apply severe fines to a company or even force it to shut down until violations have been fixed. Given the severity of these sanctions, the buyer should investigate the amount of outstanding fines, as well as the cost needed to fix underlying safety issues, and reduce the acquiree's valuation by this amount prior to settling on a final price.

Logistics Issues

1. *Determine the type of manufacturing planning system being used.* If it is not a manufacturing resources planning (MRP II) or just-in-time (JIT) system, then the buyer can install either of these systems, which will streamline the flow of inventory through the company, thereby reducing its investment in inventory and costs related to product scrap. If this is done, the buyer must budget for a substantial investment in installing the new systems, which will be offset by a reduction in the investment in all forms of inventory.

2. *Determine the investment in transport equipment.* If the buyer can cost-justify a switch to third-party shipping, then it can liquidate some or all of the transportation equipment of the acquiree, which not only results in a considerable cash inflow, but also eliminates the expense of the freight routing staff and vehicle drivers, as well as added transportation insurance costs, licensing, and vehicle taxes.

3. *Determine the locations and investments in all distribution warehouses.* The buyer can use this information to determine the savings that can be garnered by closing some warehouses in favor of a more centralized distribution pattern.

Management Issues

1. *Interview the acquiree's management team.* The buyer must know the level of experience and overall quality of the management team it is buying as part of the acquisition, so that it can determine which people to let go and which ones to retain. Without this information, it may let the wrong people go or retain managers who are not capable of improving operations to any considerable degree.

2. *Review the salary levels and employment contracts of key employees.* The buyer should know if there are significant long-term payments it is contractually obligated to pay to key employees of the acquiree, or if pay levels are excessively high or low, so that it can adjust pay levels upward for those employees it wishes to keep or reduce the business valuation by the cost of obligatory future payments to employees.

3. *Determine the benefits given to employees of the acquiree.* There can be a significant employee morale issue if the employees of the acquiree and the buyer find out that their benefit packages differ substantially from each other. If the buyer finds it necessary to scale back the benefits offered to the employees of the acquiree, then it should be prepared to experience an increased rate of employee turnover at that company, as those employees leave who were dependent on the enhanced level of benefits.

4. *Is the facility unionized?* This can be either a blessing or a problem, depending on the buyer's experience with unions. If the acquiree has had significant labor relations problems with its unions, but the buyer is more experienced in smoothing over troubled relations, then the buyer may be able to improve the performance of employees who belong to the unions, thereby increasing company profitability. However, if the buyer has no experience with unions, the reverse situation may occur; in addition, the unions whose employees work for the acquiree may even be tempted to organize the employees at the buying company's other locations.

Manufacturing Issues

1. *Determine the recent trend line of machine utilization.* This is very useful information for determining if any machines are so infrequently used that they can be sold. Alternatively, high utilization may indicate the need for substantial additional investments in equipment in the near future, which the buyer will have to fund. Also, be sure to group this information by types of related machines, so that it is easier to determine whether similar machines will still be available to take on additional work if selected machines are sold.

2. *Determine which machines are required to produce the products that contribute the most to the acquiree's gross margin.* With this information in hand, the buyer will know what types of machines to purchase in order to ensure that the most profitable sales will not be lost when machinery breaks down. Alternatively, it tells the buyer what backup machinery *not* to buy, if they are for unprofitable products.

3. *What are the types and ages of machines being used?* The buyer must know if any machines are of a type that is subject to high maintenance, or if they are too old

to be used much longer. In either case, the result may be large expenditures to replace the machines with newer ones that are also subject to less maintenance. Obtaining the maintenance records for each machine can be of great assistance in determining which ones are the most expensive to keep operational.

4. *What proportion of the production facility is being used?* If there is a significant amount of space not being used, or if the sale of some equipment will free up space, then the buyer may be able to sell off or sublease that space.

5. *What types of automation are currently being used or installed?* If there is little automation, this can represent a significant opportunity for the buyer to install such equipment, thereby driving down variable costs. However, if automation is being installed and is not yet complete, then inquire into the time period over which the installation has been proceeding. A lengthy install period can indicate trouble with the new systems that the buyer will have to resolve.

Sales Issues

1. *Are there agreements with customers that allow the acquiree to change its product prices as underlying raw material prices change?* This is a great boon to the buyer if such agreements exist, because the buyer will be protected from profit reductions that are caused by raw material price fluctuations. If not, then the buyer may have to allocate extra time to meet with customers to formulate these agreements (if the industry is one in which such agreements are commonly accepted by customers).

2. *Have any customers or prospective customers asked the acquiree to expand its product line or geographic distribution?* If so, the buying company needs to know the extent of demand for the acquiree's products, so that it can budget for an expansion of either the product line or geographic distribution system.

3. *Have there been any recent product recalls?* If so, verify that the target company has created an adequate reserve for the cost of future product returns. Also, if there is a history of product recalls, there may be significant product design issues rooted in the engineering department that will result in similar recalls for products that have not yet been released. Further, if any of the product recall problems may result in liability lawsuits, the potential legal costs of the situation may scuttle the entire acquisition deal.

4. *What are the unit sales volumes by product for the last year and the current projections for the upcoming year?* The company must know which products are on a sales decline, so that the management team can estimate the cost required to either replace them with new products or enhance the existing products or reposition them in the marketplace.

5. *What customer agreements "lock in" pricing for fixed time periods?* If a customer agreement involves a price that is well below the market price, be sure to calculate the total loss from this arrangement and reduce the purchase price by this amount. Alternatively, the purchase price may *increase* if there are customer agreements that do the reverse—lock them into high prices for some future period. These agreements are most common in the mining industry, such as between coal mines and utilities.

6. *What is the commission structure?* If the sales staff has been promised major bonus deals if they meet their sales targets, the target company could incur a major commission-related expense before the sales period is completed. Also, altering such lucrative arrangements can result in significant turnover in the sales department, which can be a problem if the sales staff is an experienced one.

7. *What is the geographic customer concentration?* This information tells the buyer whether the acquiree's facilities are appropriately situated to provide the best possible service to customers, not only in terms of warehouse locations, but also in regard to where the sales staff is based. This information may result in changes in the locations of the sales staff. A further issue is that the acquiree has a better chance of profitably replacing any distributors (who receive special discounts) in high-sales-volume areas with an in-house sales staff.

8. *What is the profitability by customer?* This is extremely critical information for a buyer, since it needs to know if there are customers who are so profitable that they should be given extra service in order to ensure their retention, as well as the existence of low-margin customers who should be dropped so that the acquiree's staff can focus on more profitable customers.

9. *What is the seasonality of sales by product line?* The sales staff of the buying company needs to know how to budget for the sales of an acquiree, so this information is necessary for that task. Also, the sales activity of the acquiree's sales staff, in terms of what times of year they push sales of some product lines the hardest, is necessary information for the buyer, because it must also schedule the same types of seasonal sales activity.

10. *What type of distributor network does the acquiree have?* This network should supplement the acquiree's own sales network, so that all major geographic areas are covered. Also, make note of the discounts granted to the distributors, to determine the amount of profits that are lost by selling to them. In addition, make note of the sales levels to each distributor, which is some indication of the sales ability of each distributor. This information will tell the buyer if the distribution network requires revamping.

Though the list in Figure 8.2 may seem like an inordinately long one, an acquiring company must be as certain as possible of the underlying fundamentals of any business it wishes to acquire so that it values the purchase correctly. Ignoring some of the steps noted here may be acceptable if the steps being discarded are clearly irrelevant to the target company under review. However, the management team must be careful about what review items are ignored, because a key cost or liability may be hidden in any of the items noted here and could result in a major overvaluation of an acquisition candidate. Thus, when in doubt about the need for some due diligence steps, it is best to err on the side of caution and complete them, although it may take extra time and money to do so.

Summary

There are many reasons for needing to place a value on the business— sale of part of the business, establishment of an ESOP, estate and gift tax planning, settlement of a divorce, or death of a principal.

Valuation methods have been very much influenced and guided by Internal Revenue Service Ruling 59–60. The ruling acknowledges that valuation is in the mind of the beholder and each case must be governed by the facts at hand without the application of a specific formula. In determining a value under this ruling, consideration should be given to eight factors:

1. The nature and history of the business
2. The economic outlook for the economy and the business specifically
3. The financial condition of the business
4. The earning capacity
5. The dividend-paying capacity
6. The amount of goodwill or tangible value
7. The sales of stock
8. Market price of comparable businesses

A discounted cash flow method of valuation may be used if the business has a limited-life income stream. Another method frequently used is an earnings capitalization approach, which is similar in financial appearance to a method used to value an insurance annuity contract. Two things are necessary: a comparison return for competing investments and a risk differential. The method is relatively simple but does not resolve how to adjust the income for certain tax and other considerations.

A method used for publicly traded companies is the price/earnings multiple method, used where the stock has a ready market value, reported earnings do not have to be significantly adjusted, and there are two comparable companies.

The business could be valued using the adjusted book value method. In using this approach, one undertakes to determine appraised values for assets. In this approach, significant adjustments may be needed to account for the company's accounting policies and practices.

Included in Revenue Ruling 59–60 is a method of valuation using the dividend paying capacity of the business over some period of time. When this method is used, some factors may be considered: working capital needs, expansion and growth cash needs, contingency needs, debt, and salaries paid to owners. By using the dividend-paying capacity and an appropriate yield, one can approximate value.

Finally, comparable businesses can be used to determine value. Finding truly comparable businesses requires comparisons of such factors as size, earnings, and the nature of the business itself. Valuation is the best guess of what the business is worth. It can only be approximated. The methods given here, however, should group several estimates within an acceptable range from which the worth of the business can be determined.

Chapter 9

Special Issues for the Rapidly Growing Company

Many entrepreneurs feel fortunate just to survive the first few years of their company's existence with a minimum of cash drain, a modest increase in sales, and some market presence. However, other entrepreneurs, either through design or sheer luck, find sales exploding and customers demanding enormous shipment quantities, as well as visits from bankers who are either offering more funds or wondering why the company cannot pay for its existing debts. If managed properly, these sudden periods of startling growth can result in the creation of enormous fortunes or the reverse—a sudden failure due to an inability to handle the growth that is evidenced by poor controls, slipshod manufacturing, spiraling costs, missed ship dates, and the worst problem of all: no cash. In this chapter, we review the benefits and related dangers of rapid growth, as well as the reasons for sudden growth spurts. We then describe the systems that a company should install to handle rapid growth situations, and conclude with a review of the growth issues that arise for each of the major departmental areas.

The Perils and Rewards of Rapid Growth

The chief reward from a sudden boost in sales is that profits can skyrocket, yielding enormous paper profits for stockholders. This happens because a company's fixed costs are already covered by existing sales, so that each additional dollar of sales creates an inordinate additional profit. This profit increases the earnings per share, which increases the value of the stock and allows shareholders to sell their shares for considerable gains. The potential reward from this type of rapid sales boost is the reason so many brokerage analysts are constantly scouring the field of publicly held companies, trying to guess which one will next be subject to a sudden run-up in sales.

Opposing the cash rewards to be gained from sudden growth are significant risks in the areas of cash flow, controls, human resources, and systems:

- *Cash flow.* When sales increase, a company must invest in additional accounts receivable, since most customers purchase on credit. For example, if the level of accounts receivable turnover is 12 turns per year, and sales increase by $1 million per month, then a company will be forced to permanently invest an additional $1 million in its accounts receivable to fund this growth. Also, if a company is in the manufacturing field, it will be selling products that require some inventory to be kept on hand. The proportion of inventory to sales will probably stay the same when sales increase, so that management must invest more funds in inventory, much as was the case for accounts receivable. Some of this investment will be offset by an increase in accounts payable, but there will be an overall jump in the investment in these areas. Also, if production or staff facilities are overwhelmed by the sales volume, then there must be an added investment in production or staff facilities, not to mention the related overhead costs that coincide with an increase in facilities. All of these factors will result in an increase in cash requirements that may very well give a company a negative cash flow, even though it is recording a profit on its income statement.
- *Controls.* When a company goes through a sudden surge in sales, the staff is overwhelmed by the transaction volume and has a very difficult time processing transactions in an orderly manner. Instead, it resorts to shortcuts to complete work as rapidly as possible, which can short-circuit control systems. This problem is exacerbated by the hiring of many new staff people to assist in

handling the workload, since they are untrained in company control systems. For example, an overworked credit department may offer credit to *all* new customers, since it has no time to conduct a proper credit review. Also, the purchasing staff may buy extra inventory, since it saves time to consolidate a large number of small purchases into a few large ones; however, this increases storage costs and the risk of inventory obsolescence. Whenever there is a control failure, a company runs the risk of incurring significant extra costs that can wipe out the profits earned by an increase in sales.

- *Human resources.* During an explosive growth surge, the human resources staff is straining to fill new positions. To do so, it may have to lower its standards and hire employees who are less productive than those currently on the payroll. This results in an incremental reduction in the efficiency of the total workforce, so that more employees are required to process each dollar of sales volume at the higher level than were previously needed at lower levels.

- *Systems.* The systems that were created to handle a lower level of transaction volume may become difficult to use, or simply collapse under the pressure imposed by a much higher sales volume. For example, a personal computer (PC) based accounting and manufacturing computer system that has been accessed by 10 users may not have adequate response times if the number of users suddenly jumps to 100 and may require replacement by a much more powerful system. Similarly, nearly any paper-based system, such as is commonly found in the sales quoting, engineering, and inventory tracking areas, is difficult to maintain at higher transaction volumes and should be replaced by a computer-based system. If a company has too many of these antiquated systems in key operating areas, then it may find that it is incapable of meeting customer orders in a timely manner. The required system changes may be so extensive that their cost grossly exceeds any additional profits to be gained from a jump in sales.

Given the possible severity of the problems that must be overcome before a company can benefit from a sharp gain in sales volume, it is critical for the management team to understand the reasons for sudden jumps in sales volume (as noted in the next section), so that it can more properly prepare for them.

The Reasons for Sudden Growth Spurts

A sudden jump in sales is most commonly found in companies that have discovered a new market and are the first ones to deliver a product in that market. If there is a significant amount of pent-up demand, then the company originating the product will be deluged with orders. However, this is not an easy sales boost to predict, because the sales level in an entirely new market is exceedingly difficult to determine in advance, with the sales staff having to rely on marketing surveys regarding the expectations of possible customers to buy the product at various price points, which may be inaccurate.

Another reason for a growth spurt is a company's dropping the price of its product by a substantial amount or using a short-term sales promotion that has the same result. This phenomenon has been occurring in the PC industry for years. The reason for the price drop may be an explicit desire to reach a new group of customers who will not buy at a higher price point, or it may be intended to steal existing market share away from a competitor whose product has a higher price. Once again, however, the resulting increase in sales is extremely difficult to predict, especially if the lower price point increases the overall size of the market, because no one knows the extent to which the market will now expand.

Another reason for a jump in sales is a fad. A fad may be sparked by an innovative advertising campaign, a public event that is widely publicized, or through promotion by a powerful group of opinion leaders. Whatever the case may be, fads tend to result in sudden and enormous increases in sales, followed by an equally sudden drop back to previous or lower levels once the fad is over. Neither the timing of a fad nor its extent can be estimated with any reliability.

Yet another reason for explosive growth is a deliberate growth strategy that results in inordinate sales gains. This can be through a calculated attempt to sell in new geographic regions or by acquiring other companies. The first of the two cases is more difficult to handle, since a company has no infrastructure with which to deal with the extra sales, whereas an acquired company is already able to handle its existing sales but may run into trouble if the acquiring company wants to alter or combine its existing systems. This type of growth results in more predictable sales than is the case with the preceding causes of growth, but still requires considerable systemic changes to properly handle.

In all of these cases except the last, a company is confronted with seemingly intractable problems—no way of knowing when a growth spurt will start or stop, nor the point at which sales will peak. Though the examples presented here represent the most extreme forms of explosive growth, most companies must deal with this situation to a lesser degree, perhaps with moderately successful new products, products with reasonable pricing, or new innovations that result in products that are mildly differentiated from those of the competition. In all these cases, management must take specific steps in advance not only to capitalize on the sudden growth, but also to forestall problems. In the following sections, we look at system-related changes that will improve a company's ability to weather the storm of rapid growth.

Cash Management Issues

As noted earlier in this chapter, rapid growth requires an investment in working capital, the prime components of which are accounts receivable and inventory. In addition, there will be fixed-asset investments in order to keep production capacity in line with sales volume. Both of these issues will result in an outflow of cash, unless profits are so extraordinarily high that all necessary investments can be funded internally. In this section, we review how to forecast cash, moderate its use, and ensure that operations spin off the largest possible amount of additional funds. A rapidly growing company must handle cash perfectly in order to survive the growth onslaught, so the controller or chief financial officer (CFO) should review this section in detail and implement all recommended changes.

The first cash management issue to resolve at once is the profitability of products and customers. If a company has no idea how much money it is making on various products or customers, then it

FIGURE 9.1

Standard Margin Analysis

Description	Price	Material Cost	Labor Cost	Overhead Cost	Direct Margin	Allocated Margin
Alarm clock	$18.00	$9.00	$5.50	$3.50	19%	0%
Luggage liner	18.50	10.00	3.50	.50	27%	24%
Luggage tag	5.75	2.00	.75	1.00	52%	35%
Passport holder	8.75	2.50	1.50	1.75	54%	34%
Power converter	12.25	6.50	2.00	2.50	31%	10%
Shoe bag	3.50	2.00	.25	.75	36%	14%
Umbrella	24.50	12.00	4.50	5.00	33%	12%

will likely allocate its resources in the wrong direction, such as more production facilities for its least profitable products or extended accounts receivable to customers from whom it makes no money. To resolve this problem, the accounting staff should first determine the standard cost of all products. Standard costs can be quickly derived from the bills of material (BOMs) for each product, and so the accounting staff can sometimes develop a list of product costs in just a few hours or days, based on this information. Then the most commonly used price point is used as the standard product price, which yields a standard gross margin for each product. When the gross margin percentage is sorted in increasing order, management has a "quick and dirty" report that tells it where there are probable margin difficulties that require either repricing or the elimination of the product. The accounting staff can then determine the gross margin by customer, simply by compiling sales by product for each customer and then using the standard costs to determine the standard margin by customer. An example of the standard margin analysis is shown in Figure 9.1, which lists the key cost components for a series of travel-related products. Note that two margins are listed; one is for the direct margin, which excludes the cost of allocated overhead, while a fully burdened margin includes it. These two different margins allow management to see if it is making money *prior to* any additional cost allocation—if not, the product must either be terminated or repriced at once, for the company is losing money on every unit sold.

After the standard margin analysis is complete, the accounting team should go back and verify that the BOM quantities are accurate, and add any other variances to the analysis, such as scrap and labor variances. It can also conduct an activity-based costing analysis, which is a very careful and detailed method for allocating overhead costs to products and customers. These extra steps will add to the accuracy of the standard margin numbers, but take so long to develop that the information will probably not be available to the management team until well into a sales run-up, when it may be too late to take action on the resulting margin information. Consequently, the accounting staff should always release the standard margin information first, and then issue a second and more accurate set of information, based on additional data, as soon thereafter as possible.

Using the gross margin report, management should eliminate all products and customers who do not return the largest possible margin. Even those returning a small or modest margin should be eliminated. The reason for reducing the product and customer mix down to only the most profitable is that exceptional growth requires investments in accounts receivable, inventory, and fixed assets, and all these investments are best supported through cash that is generated internally—and a sufficient amount of cash can be generated only with the highest-margin products. If the management team discovers that the bulk of its new sales growth is in low-margin products, it should seriously consider if it is worthwhile to grow at all, since the low-margin sales will not spin off enough cash to support any significant amount of growth.

Having forestalled expansion through low-margin products and customers, we can now proceed to the forecasting of cash flow. This is an extremely necessary step, for management must be fully aware of when a company is dipping into its cash reserves, which may call for much advance work to add more debt or equity to support further growth. If there is no cash forecasting, then management will still have to acquire cash, but will now be forced to do so on a rush basis, which can threaten company operations, and very likely will result in less favorable lending or investment terms by lenders or investors. The basic cash forecast, such as the one shown in Figure 9.2, begins with a sales projection for the next few months and factors in the cash expenses that are likely to arise at those sales levels,

FIGURE 9.2

Sample Cash Forecast

Cash Flow Line Item	January	February	March
Section I: Assumptions			
Sales dollars per period	$2,000,000	$2,500,000	$3,000,000
Production costs as a percentage of sales	50%	55%	55%
Days needed to collect accounts receivable	45	45	45
Days needed to pay accounts payable	30	30	30
Days of inventory on hand	60	60	60
Sales tax percentage	6%	6%	6%
Sales per employee	$100,000	$100,000	$100,000
Annual average pay per employee	$40,000	$41,000	$41,500
Section II: Cash Inflows			
Collections on accounts receivable*	$2,000,000	$2,000,000	$2,250,000
Collections on notes receivable	5,000	5,000	2,500
Collections from asset sales	0	15,000	0
Collections from equity sales	0	0	100,000
Total cash inflows	$2,005,000	$2,020,000	$2,352,500
Section III: Cash Outflows			
Payments for production costs*	$1,000,000	$1,100,000	$1,375,000
Payments for salaries and wages	66,667	85,417	103,750
Payments for general and administrative costs	175,000	175,000	175,000
Payments for capital expenditures	0	150,000	0
Payments for notes payable	25,000	25,000	25,000
Payments for sales taxes	120,000	150,000	180,000
Payments for income taxes	0	0	75,000
Payments for dividends	0	0	200,000
Incremental inventory change	0	750,000	550,000
Total cash outflows	$1,386,667	$2,435,417	$2,683,750
Net Cash Flows	+618,333	−415,417	−331,250
Cumulative Net Cash Flows	$+618,333	$202,916	$−128,334

* Sales for each of the two preceding months are assumed to be $2,000,000.
Reprinted with permission from Steven Bragg, *The Controller's Guide to Financial Analysis* (New York: John Wiley & Sons, 2000).

plus changes in working capital and fixed-asset investments during the forecasted period. There will also be forecasted cash receipts and disbursement from prior periods, since billings from preceding periods may not be collected for a few months thereafter, with accounts payable following the same track. The bottom line of the cash forecast should note the amount of cash shortfall or surplus for each forecasted period, as well as the cumulative shortfall or surplus for the entire range of forecasted periods, which the CFO uses to determine future funding needs.

The first release of the cash forecast will not be that accurate, because the person issuing it will not have factored in all possible variables that affect cash flow. However, the forecast can be made more precise by delving into the details of why the forecast was inaccurate in the preceding period. By investigating these issues and updating the next version of the forecast to reflect them, it can be brought up to a high level of accuracy that makes it a valuable tool for determining future cash flows.

So far in this section, we have discovered how to identify the poorest-performing products and customers, as well as create a format for forecasting cash flows. These steps give us information about the current and future state of a company's cash flows. Now we will proceed into specific steps designed to reduce a company's cash usage. The main categories treated here are working capital, capital expenditures, and other expenses:

- *Working capital.* The first component of working capital is accounts receivable. A company can reduce its investment in this area either by engaging in very active collection practices, or by reducing the amount of credit granted to customers. The first method is a good one and well worth the extra expense of more collections personnel. In some cases, tightening customer credit may also be an excellent way to eliminate those customers who buy only low-margin products, or who demand extra services that cut into a company's margins. The second component of working capital is inventory. Management can reduce its investment here by implementing an inventory planning and control system, such as material requirements planning, or a more advanced system that seeks to reduce inventory, such as just-in-time (JIT). Either approach forces a company to buy only the material it needs for immediate production requirements, thereby avoiding an excess investment in inventory. The final element of working capital is accounts payable. Suppliers will tolerate a modest lengthening of payment terms by a company, but this must not be abused, or else suppliers will stop deliveries or require cash on delivery. All these methods can help a company control its working capital investment.

- *Capital expenditures.* The capital budgeting process should be rife with review points, approvals, and measurement systems. By requiring an exceptional amount of analysis work prior to purchasing an asset, a company can find less expensive alternatives or at least delay cash expenditures. For example, there should be a rigorous cash flow analysis associated with every capital purchase, to ensure that it will generate more cash than is required to purchase it. Also, the approval of department managers, the general manager, president, and perhaps even the board of directors should be solicited, not because of any bureaucratic desire to halt the acquisition process, but rather because these people have enough experience to suggest alternatives that may save money.

- *Other expenses.* Two other areas in which a growing company should focus its attention are the use of the budget as a benchmarking tool, and staffing levels. The budget is usually a reflection of actual historical costs that have been adjusted for expected sales volumes, and extended forward into the current period. Because of its factual basis, this is an excellent tool for comparison to actual results. The accounting staff should use it to create a comparison of budgeted to actual costs for all expense line items, which should also include the name of the responsible manager. This report must then be walked through the company to ensure that everyone is aware of budget variances, which keeps a tight focus on meeting the targeted expense levels.

Staffing is an area that regularly runs out of control during rapid growth periods. One way to control it is to establish a historically based sales level per employee, and keep the sales-to-employee ratio at the same level as sales increase. This ratio can also be derived through benchmarking other companies, because the internal ratio may not reflect the most efficient operating history.

Another approach is to track the overtime percentage for every employee and in aggregate by department and division. This measure can be extremely revealing, because it shows which employees are continually using too much overtime, as well as those areas that can save money by replacing overtime hours with regular hours worked by new employees.

In this section, we have described how to improve a company's ability to internally generate cash, as well as forecast future cash balances, and then reviewed methods for improving its ability to manage its cash flows. These are essential steps that a rapidly growing company must master in order to ensure its survival. However, they should not be used just by companies that are on a fast growth track. These cash-related issues are helpful for all companies, because they force management to maintain tight control over a company's cash inflows and outflows.

Control Issues

Good controls can greatly assist a growing company, because they ensure the smooth flow of transactions in the manner specified in the company's policies and procedures manual, which are designed to protect company assets.

There are two kinds of controls that a growing company must concern itself with. One is control over items that can keep it from growing, while the other is control over those processes that are actively driving growth. One example of the first type of control is an uninterruptible power supply, which keeps a company's computers running in the event of a power failure. Without it, the computers could crash, which would keep the company from conducting any business. Other similar controls are data backups and disaster recovery planning, both of which are designed to keep a company's computing capability up and running during business hours.

The latter type of control, which is over those processes that drive growth, will vary depending on the type of growth strategy that a company has adopted. For example, if a company is growing by acquiring other companies, then it must focus on the pace at which it is acquiring new companies (too fast, and it cannot integrate them properly into existing operations; too slow, and investors may not be happy), the average time needed to integrate each one into other parts of the company, and the costs to acquire and transition each one. These are the key control points on which the management team must focus in order to ensure an orderly increase in the rate of growth that does not result in runaway costs or lower-than-expected revenue results.

Another type of sales growth is through a rapid product creation and rollout process, as is practiced by such standout companies as 3M, Nike, and Sony. They all strive to be the first to market with new product designs and follow them up with a nearly infinite number of product variations and add-on components, all priced to yield high margins. In this type of growth strategy, key controls should be over the time needed to bring a product to market and the capacity of the engineering staff to produce an increasing stream of new product designs, as well as its ability to meet a product design schedule that churns out new products at regular intervals, plus the research cost per product. These are obviously very different controls from the ones just advocated for the growth-by-acquisition strategy, but that is because the key success factors have changed to the speed and cost of new product rollouts.

A final growth strategy is that of expanding sales into new territories. This approach is used by any retail operation, such as Nordstrom or Burger King, when it constructs new stores in geographic areas where it has not sold before. Under this approach, the controls must closely target customer complaints, the speed with which new stores are added, new store sales levels and growth rates, and the ability of the corporate logistics system to support product shipments to the new locations. The intent of these controls is to ensure that sales levels at the new locations are meeting expectations.

In this section, we have focused on creating very specific control points that are tailored to a company's growth strategy. If a company does not follow this approach, then it may find itself spending an inordinate amount of resources controlling the wrong activities, which will have little bearing on a company's ability to succeed in its chosen growth strategy.

Management and Ownership Issues

In this section, we review the types of managers and management responsibilities that work best in an explosive growth environment.

At the top of the organizational structure sit the "Chief" officers—the chief executive officer (CEO), chief operating officer (COO), and chief financial officer (CFO). The skills of all three must be tailor-made for a rapid growth situation. The CEO should have previous experience in a high-growth situation, with tremendous planning skills, so that he or she can anticipate growth-related problems, and deal with them before they become major issues. In addition, if a company is growing by acquisition, it is the CEO's responsibility to set up the acquisition process and either lead or assist in the negotiation of purchases of other companies.

The COO is in charge of corporate operations, and in this role must have a strong understanding of all major functional areas, so that this person can prowl through the company, spotting and correcting problem areas before they become major issues. Also, given the extraordinary rate at which a company must expand its operations during an explosive growth period, the COO must also be willing to delegate large chunks of control to a cadre of lower-level managers, which alters this person's job from that of a detail-oriented manager to one who not only monitors business conditions but also trains and mentors many other managers.

The CFO must be an expert in the analysis of cash flows and the procurement of additional debt and equity. This person does not need to be an expert in operational accounting, since the controller takes care of that work. This position must be entirely concerned with the rate at which the company is using up cash, the sources from which cash can be expected, and the timing of any shortfalls. This is an exceptionally critical position in a growth situation, and a weakness here can doom a growing company.

Below these top three positions lie the middle-management ranks, which must be staffed with managers of the highest possible quality. The reason for the high level of required excellence here is that, since the company is constantly expanding its employee base, this group is also called on, in a manner similar to that of the COO, to delegate authority even further down into the organization, which means that each of these people must become a "mini" COO, with excellent recruiting, training, and mentoring skills, not to mention an in-depth knowledge of the operations under their immediate control.

As previously noted, rapid growth necessitates a great deal of delegation to lower levels within an organization. This can be a problem for senior management teams that are used to centralized decision making. That approach is no longer viable in an explosive growth situation, because a vast number of decisions must be made in all functional areas in order to support the ongoing growth rate; if the senior management group insists on approving all these decisions, then it will become the bottleneck that keeps the company from growing—there are simply too many decisions to make, and there is not enough time for a few senior managers to investigate and approve them all. Consequently, a growing company must alter its overall management style to push decision making as far down into the ranks of the company as possible. This approach results in quick decisions that allow a company to grow at a faster rate, but also carries with it some risk of financial loss if the wrong decisions are made. Consequently, the senior management team should spend a great deal of time determining the types of decisions that lower levels of management will be allowed to authorize, with particular attention to the mitigation of financial risks.

If lower-level managers are to make reasonable decisions, they must also be given access to a sufficient amount of operational and financial information; otherwise, they will not have enough background information to make the right decisions. Handing out this information can be a hard change in operating philosophy for those senior management teams that believe in centralizing and protecting such information. Instead, they must now accustom themselves to disseminating both budgeted and actual financial information, not to mention a variety of operational statistics. Though this can be a difficult transition, the management team will find that lower-level managers will make better decisions, which generally results in a second bonus—reduced turnover in the management ranks because there is more job satisfaction.

A final point regarding management issues is the span of control. This is the average number of employees that each manager is expected to supervise. Historically, the span of control has been roughly seven employees per manager, though this can vary significantly for different positions, organizational structures, and industries. When a company enters a rapid growth phase, senior management is frequently unable to hire a sufficient number of new managers to keep the span of control at its traditional level, which results in a very overworked group of managers who must now oversee far more people than was previously the case. However, this is only a short-term solution, for the overextended managers will eventually burn out and leave the company, thereby contributing to a further degradation in the span of control. Instead, a company should either endeavor to retain the old span of control, even if it means curtailing the rate of growth, or else use some entirely new organizational structure that reduces the management time per employee of each manager.

In summary, the best management structure in a rapidly growing company is one in which senior management pushes as much decision-making authority as possible down into the lower management ranks, along with a large amount of key financial and operational information that lower managers will use to make better decisions. This can be a revolutionary management philosophy for the more centralized organizations, and if not dealt with at the beginning of a growth surge, will probably hinder or stop the rate of growth.

Ownership Issues

The owner of a rapidly growing business may find that the problems associated with the growth rate are larger than the benefits to be gained through a higher stock price. In this section, we cover the more common problems that an owner must face.

One of the most prevalent issues for an owner is that, as outlined in the preceding section, a rapidly growing firm needs only the best managers, which may require the replacement of a group of long-term and faithful managers who simply do not possess the skills needed to take a company to the next level of sales growth. This is a particular problem if the managers are old friends or people to whom an owner feels some particular obligation. There are several ways to deal with this problem. One is large severance packages to those managers who must be replaced, which certainly eases the pain of separation. Another option is to give them responsible positions in functional areas of the company that are not so critical to key operations. A third option for those current managers who show some growth potential is to pair them with new managers, so that they can watch and learn, and hopefully take up responsible (though perhaps lesser) roles in the newer and larger corporation. However, this last option is a difficult one, because the old managers are in a unique position to observe and criticize their replacements. A mix of all three options may be the best approach, depending on the mix of personalities and skills in the group of mangers being replaced.

Another problem is loss of control. When a company grows at a rapid rate, it requires a great deal of cash to support the higher levels of working capital, fixed assets, and overhead that go along with the higher sales volume. An owner may not have the cash to pay for this out of personal resources, and so the owner is confronted with two difficult choices. One is to greatly increase the amount of financial leverage by taking on a large amount of debt, which carries with it the risk of default, since lenders will be able to demand the liquidation of collateral that is pledged against new loans, which can result in corporate bankruptcy. A potentially equally unpalatable option is to sell shares in the company to other investors, which will weaken an owner's control over the company. One option for dealing with this situation is for an owner to sell nonvoting shares of common stock, though these will be worth less on the open market, due to their lack of voting control. Another approach is to sell shares down to the point where the owner still retains 50.1 percent of all shares, which still results in voting control. Finally, an owner may sell out to other investors, rather than tolerate co-ownership of the firm.

If an owner sells share to a limited group of investors or to the public at large, this may also result in great differences in the way the owner is allowed to use the company. In the past, the owner may have tapped the corporate till to pay the salaries of family members, as well as for company cars, planes, and various personal expenses. However, when a corporation is owned by a larger group, the former sole owner must now behave in a manner that results in the highest possible returns for the entire investment group, which will likely result in a decline in the number or size of extra benefits taken.

A final ownership issue is the degree of management control that the owner should take over the newly expanded organization. In the past, the owner may have preferred an extreme degree of micromanagement, which was more appropriate during the company's infancy, when systems and controls were poor. However, with an experienced and talented management team in place, this is no longer appropriate, because employees do not know who is running the company—the management group or the owner. Instead, the owner should satisfy his or her issues with systems and controls by chairing the audit committee, which authorizes specific types of internal audits and reviews the results. The owner should also review operating and financial results with other members of the board of directors and direct the management team to alter its operational or strategic direction in accordance with those results. In short, the owner must move up to the top of the organization and stay there—roving through and changing the organization "on the fly" is no longer acceptable behavior.

Thus, the owner faces many wrenching changes as a result of fast growth. There may be a complete replacement of the top management team, as well as a loss of control over the company or a higher level of financial risk, as well as a stepping back from daily operations. Because this is such a new role for an owner, many owners feel uncomfortable and instead sell their shares and leave the company.

Partnership and Joint Venture Issues

A rapidly growing company rarely has the resources to erect a comprehensive set of production facilities, sell the resulting products in every market around the world, or properly service the needs of customers thereafter. There simply is not enough cash, nor are there enough qualified employees to attack every possible opportunity. In many cases, growing companies cannot address every market opportunity, and so must settle for a lower level of sales and service. One way to solve this dilemma is the use of partnerships and joint ventures.

Under these arrangements, two or more companies pool their resources to achieve an end result, such as the development of a new product, the production of a new facility, or co-ownership of a new marketing entity. In these cases, there is no customer-to-supplier relationship, but rather a partnership in which the co-owners share both the risks and rewards, though these may be in differing proportions, usually in relationship to the amount of investment made by each party.

A growing company should make maximum use of partnership arrangements, since it now has access to the investment funds of another company; it would not otherwise have access to this level of funding unless it increased its financial leverage by adding debt or by watering down the ownership shares of the current owners by adding equity. Under this new approach, a company has access to funds without any of the risks that are attendant on the more traditional forms of financing.

The downside of this approach is that partners want an equitable share of the profits, so that a growing company will not realize as much of a gain from a venture as it would if it had funded the entire thing itself. However, it is also possible that the growing company could not have financed the venture at all by itself, perhaps due to the sheer volume of funding needed. This is an especially common problem for biotechnology start-up companies, which have great new products but no way to invest hundreds of millions of dollars to obtain government approval, build production facilities, or create distribution systems. In this case, the usual result is a partnership with a larger drug company, in which the start-up company provides *none* of the funds but *all* of the expertise, and takes a modest share of the resulting profits. Also, a growing company must remember that all investments carry with them a risk of failure, so that by spreading the invested amount among one or more partners, a failure will not necessarily bring about the demise of the company. Thus, one must counterbalance the loss of profits against the reduced risk of loss, as well as the greater capability of the combined entities to complete major projects.

The greatest risk associated with a partnership is not of financial loss, but rather of information loss. This is because the partnering companies may be sharing confidential information as part of the venture, which either party may use to further its own ends or pass along to other companies who may use it. One can protect against this to some extent by having all parties sign confidentiality agreements, but there is no question that trade secrets will move between companies. Consequently, it is sometimes best to partner only with companies outside one's industry, so that the partners have little use for any information they may acquire.

When used appropriately, partnerships and joint ventures can be a powerful tool for extending the amount of a company's financial and intellectual resources to take on new and profitable endeavors.

Budgeting Issues

Some corporate managers may say that, because the rate of growth is so high, it is absurd to attempt to budget for it, because the results will be nowhere near the anticipated levels. To some extent, they have a point—the final revenue and expense figures may vary significantly from budgeted levels. Nonetheless, the alternative is to operate with no budget at all, which is the one document that gives some structure to the steps a company takes to deal with growth. Consequently, we advocate not only the use of a budget in this situation, but also its repeated review and updating throughout the course of the budget year. In this section, we will demonstrate the specific uses of a budget in this situation.

A key reason for using a budget in a fast-growth scenario is that one can use it to model the number of personnel in each department. For example, if past history indicates that the average salesperson can sell $1 million of product per year, then it stands to reason that the budget model should automatically calculate the pay of one additional salesperson for each additional $1 million of sales for the upcoming year, barring the use of new technology that may increase productivity. Similarly, if the accounts payable staff can handle $10 million of accounts payable transactions per person, the budget should indicate additions in this department that also link the headcount to the level of activity. This type of modeling should be adjusted for differences in assumed levels of productivity and pay rates to make it more accurate. This is an excellent way to determine approximate staffing levels in relation to activity levels.

Another reason for the budget is to estimate cash flows. This is one of the chief functions of the CFO, who must constantly update the budget with new sales, expense, and asset turnover figures to determine the best estimates of cash surpluses and (more likely) shortages, which are then used to determine funding requirements. Without a budget model that generates cash flow projections, the CFO must create a simplified budget model just to estimate cash flows, so having the budget model eliminates this extra work by the CFO.

A budget can also be used to track a company's performance against its specific type of growth strategy. For example, a strategy to grow by adding stores in new territories should call for a budget that is structured by single-store revenues and expenses, so that one can easily compare it to actual results for new stores to determine any variances. Similarly, a strategy to grow by new product introductions requires a budget format that estimates sales and revenues for each new product to be released. The next step is to create a variance report that compares each new growth element (e.g., a new store or a new product) to actual results for the same units of measure. For example, if 10 new stores were opened, then there should be a separate page in the variance report for each store, showing the variances from budget for all line items. If there are significant differences in results over the first few months of operation, it may also be necessary to construct a trend line of results for the most important budget line items, which management can track to ensure that revenues or expenses are gradually achieving their desired levels.

Finally, the budget can be used to construct "what if" scenarios. This is an extremely fruitful way to use a budget model, because a rapidly growing company is not certain of its exact future, and should constantly review all possible scenarios with which it may be confronted. To use "what if" scenarios, a budget model should be tied to a small number of key variables, such as percentage changes in the revenue growth rate, the inflation rate, or changes in the price of key products. Altering any of these key variables will automatically change the budget, so that revenues and expenses are altered to reflect the new assumptions. To use this approach properly, the finance staff should conduct extensive modeling, so that the management team is adequately informed regarding both best-case and worst-case scenarios. The finance team and the management group as a whole should also work together to assign probabilities to the likelihood of attaining each of the various scenarios, which gives it a good basis on which to modify operating and financial decisions. If the rate of sales growth changes, then the finance group should continue to revise its budget scenarios to reflect the new information. If this calls for a new budget analysis every month, then so be it—the management team must be given the most accurate budget scenarios, or it cannot properly manage the business.

Thus, the budget is an effective tool for managing a rapidly growing business. The main differences between the use of a budget in slow-growth and fast-growth environments are the increased number of budget iterations required and its use as a scenario analysis tool.

Department Issues

In each of the major corporate departments, there are specific activities that must be completed for a rapidly growing company to survive, as well as other tasks that are not only of no use in such situations but may be detrimental. In this section, we will quickly review these key factors for each of the most important corporate functions, so that a management team knows what tasks it must accomplish and which ones to avoid.

In the accounting department, the focus should be on cash flow and margin analysis. As noted earlier, margin analysis is a continuing cost accounting function that involves the determination of gross margins for products and customers, so that the management team knows which products and customers to concentrate its sales efforts on, thereby creating more positive cash flow to feed the expenses of the growing company. However, cash flow issues are not confined to the study of gross margins. The accounting staff must also send out invoices to customers as soon as possible after product shipment, and by the quickest means (such as electronic billings), so that funds will be paid by customers much sooner. For the same reason, the collections function must be very well run and aggressive in collecting overdue funds. This effort is aided by reducing billing errors, since this is a prime reason why customers do not pay on time. Also, there should be a tightly managed cash collection system using lockboxes, so that receipts from customers are deposited as soon as possible, thereby allowing for the shortest possible time period that a company is funding its accounts receivable. Finally, the accounts payable staff must be sure to never pay a supplier invoice earlier than is absolutely necessary, because such an action will reduce the amount of cash on hand. All of these actions by the accounting department are tightly focused on improving the flow of cash.

Nearly all activities handled by the accounting department must be completed at some point, but it is possible to either slow down or reduce the frequency of some activities, so that greater efforts can be focused on actions needed to improve cash flow. For example, the number of payroll periods can be dropped from once a week to once or twice a month, which cuts down the time needed to process transactions through the payroll system. Another possibility is to outsource selected functions, such as tax form processing or payroll processing, which also frees up staff for activities more precisely targeted at improving cash flows.

The internal audit department must focus on those activities that will have the greatest impact on cash flows and the incurring of unnecessary expenses (which also affects cash flow). One such area is the revenue cycle, where audits should focus on the accuracy and timing of shipment and invoicing transactions, to ensure that billings are correctly processed in a timely manner for 100 percent of shipments. Similarly, the internal audit staff should review the purchasing cycle to verify that only authorized items are being purchased, that purchase prices are reasonable, that excessive quantities are not being purchased for inventory (since this would represent an excessive cash investment in inventory), and that supplier payments are being correctly processed. Finally, the auditors should verify that cash is being properly recorded and invested. All of these actions are tightly focused on maintaining systems that flawlessly marshal the flow of cash-related transactions both in and out of a company.

The main chores of the computer services department in an explosive-growth environment are to ensure that the key computer systems do not fail (which could bring all operations to a halt) and the dissemination of key operating and financial information throughout the company through special reports on executive information systems (a key aspect of delegating decision making down into an organization, as discussed in the management section). One of the best ways to ensure good computer "up time" is to use only "plain vanilla" packaged software that has been extensively debugged and tested by a supplier. This type of software crashes much less frequently than fancy, custom-designed programs. Also, the department should install uninterruptible power supplies for all computers, as well as long-term backup power generators, both of which will keep computer systems operational in the event of an external power failure. Also, there should be a regularly reviewed disaster recovery plan that includes daily backups and off-site tape storage, as well as an off-site computer processing center that acts in a backup role. As for the communication objective, the computer services staff should create corporate intranets that allow for the posting of key information in network locations where users can easily access it. Another approach is to install an executive information system that pulls in data from a variety of company databases and presents it to users in a number of trend lines, ratios, and charts that clearly show operational and financial problem areas. Conversely, the computer services staff should not become bogged down in the development of custom programming projects, because these tend to draw resources away from the more important objectives just outlined.

The customer service department takes a lead role when there is a sales surge, because this function interacts with all the newly acquired customers, and is in a good position not only to lock in customer loyalty, but also to glean from them any problems with company products, services, or systems. Because of its primary position, there are several tasks on which this group must concentrate its efforts. One is to maintain a database of customer complaints, to which other parts of the company have ready access. This tells everyone what service or product areas are in need of improvement, as well as the company's response time in getting back to the customer. Further, the staff must use this database to resolve customer problems as soon as possible, so that there is a reduced risk of losing valuable customers. Also, the department should focus on rapid responses to customers in all areas of communication—not only in regard to their complaints, but also for the status of their orders, such as production and shipment dates. The highest degree of communication with customers will improve their satisfaction with the service provided by the company, which assists greatly in retaining them for a long time. Finally, the customer service manager must focus on hiring and training the best possible customer service employees. This is an area that does not always attract people with the highest service motivation or communication skills, which is a real danger when these employees are the primary contact points between customers and the company.

The distribution function is one that many companies ignore, but this can be a fatal error for a growing company to make. A great deal of cash may be invested in a distribution system that is not efficiently organized, and that is cash that a growing company can more profitably use elsewhere. One goal to focus on is an improvement in the rate of inventory turnover, which can be enhanced through an accurate inventory tracking system, just-in-time purchases, and accurate BOMs from which parts are ordered. Another target is a reduction in the number of stocking points. For example, if a company elects to create warehouses for finished goods and spare parts that are near every major customer, then it must realize that this will require an investment in a complete set of inventory items at every one of those locations; a better approach is to either create a smaller number of large regional warehouses or use express delivery from a single location. Another issue is to reduce the number of unique product configurations, since each one requires some finished inventory to be kept in stock, which represents an additional investment in inventory. Two alternate approaches are to deliberately eliminate a number of the slowest-selling product configurations or to keep them all, but conduct final assembly at the point of distribution, because this allows a company to maintain inventory of a smaller number of component parts that can then be configured in a variety of different ways. Finally, a company can liquidate its investment in its own distribution systems by selling its trucking fleet and outsourcing shipments to independent freight carriers, as well as by avoiding an investment in very expensive automated storage and retrieval systems. These are all excellent ways to reduce the cash invested in a company's distribution system.

Like all departments, the engineering staff can take steps to improve company cash flow. In this functional area, the engineers have a direct impact on a company's investment in inventory, which it affects in two ways. One is that the engineers should design finished products to have the smallest number of new component parts, which allows the purchasing staff to maintain a smaller investment in raw materials inventory, because this keeps the number of stockable parts to the lowest level. Also, they should design products with the smallest number of configurations, so that there are fewer versions of finished goods inventory to keep in stock; unfortunately, the engineers sometimes have little control over this item, since the marketing department may request all of the product configurations! In addition, the engineering staff should release an accurate BOM with all of its new designs, so that the purchasing staff knows precisely what parts to buy for production of those designs. Without this information, the purchasing staff must guess at what it is buying, which results in an extra cash investment in the wrong types of inventory. All of these engineering actions are targeted at improving a growing company's cash flow.

Besides cash flow, the engineering staff has another goal that is critical in a rapidly growing company—that of issuing new products at a prodigious rate. This goal is most applicable to those companies that have a specific strategy of growth by issuing new products (as opposed to those that grow by acquisition or territorial expansion, since their product emphasis is much lower). To issue products rapidly, the engineering staff should focus on designing from a common platform whenever possible. For example, Ford Motor Company uses the same car platform for both its Jaguar and Lincoln cars, which saves it a great deal of design work. Similarly, there should be an electronic design library on hand, which engineers can use to select parts to include in their newest designs. The library only includes those parts that have been tested and approved for use in company products and also includes the complete specifications of each item, which can be "cut and pasted" directly into the electronic designs for new products. Further, the engineering staff should avoid the continual enhancement of existing products with new parts, since this will require the stocking of new parts (and the possible write-off of old parts in stock that will no longer be used), which requires an additional cash investment. Also, there should be multidisciplinary teams assigned to the production of each new product, so that problems can be resolved more quickly, which results in a more rapid design process. Finally, a dedicated team of engineers should be assigned to investigate and repair all problems with existing products as expeditiously as possible, so that revenues will not suffer too much from a design flaw. All of these recommendations are designed to create a steady flow of products that will spur revenue growth and are particularly important for those companies that rely on new products to sustain their growth.

The finance staff has a unique role in a growing company that extends beyond those cash management tasks required of the accounting staff. It must also carefully forecast cash flows in the near term and constantly update this information, so that management is fully aware of the timing and extent of future cash shortfalls. The finance staff must also negotiate lines of credit and longer-term forms of debt as far in advance as possible, while also maintaining relations with investors who may be willing to invest additional funds into the company on short notice. The finance staff can also influence cash flows by its handling of the amounts of credit granted to customers. This should be relatively tight, since a company cannot afford to invest an excessive amount in its accounts receivable. To a large degree, the finance staff can control the rate of corporate growth by loosening or tightening the corporate credit granting policy, so this is a major issue that may require the involvement of other members of the management team. The finance area is one in which virtually all functions should be considered critical to the attainment of a company's rapid-growth goals.

The primary goal of the human resources department in an explosive-growth company is to recruit and train the best possible employees, and in volumes that will keep up with internal demand. This means that the staff must tap into all possible means of finding possible recruits, which calls for the use of advertisements in newspapers and targeted trade journals, as well as job postings on such Web sites as the Monster Board and Career Mosaic, plus outside recruiting firms. Some firms go so far as to advertise in movie theaters or attach advertisement streamers to airplanes and fly them around competing firms. In addition to initially finding potential employees, the human resources staff must also manage a process of testing and interviewing these recruits, to ensure that all minimum standards of experience, maturity, and skills are met. Further, the department must create and manage training programs for them, which can range from familiarization seminars to in-depth training in specialized topics. These steps ensure that a continuing stream of qualified personnel are hired who can assist a company in maintaining a high rate of growth. Also, the department should monitor the periodic job review reports of managers to see if there are employees who can be prevented from leaving by various means, such as a change of manager, shift, or benefits. Finally, even if the department is unable to retain employees, it must give them a detailed exit interview to ensure that the company is fully aware of why employees are leaving, so that it can remedy the problems and keep the outflow of employees to the smallest possible trickle. Thus, the main tasks of the human resources group in a rapid-growth environment are to meet a company's demands for new employees, while also ensuring that work conditions will not prevent current employees from leaving.

The primary goal of the manufacturing department is no different from that of the other departments in a growth situation—to contribute to overall cash flows by using the minimum amount of resources to manufacture product. One way to do this is to switch over to a material pull system, such as the JIT system used by Toyota. Under this system, no production occurs until a process farther down the production line needs a part. At this point, production is authorized to create just enough product for current needs, and then production stops until signaled to create more inventory. Though this can be a difficult system to create and maintain, it is also one that requires the smallest possible amount of raw materials, work-in-process, and finished goods inventory. One method that assists in the construction of a JIT system is the reduction of machine setup times. By doing so, management is less inclined to justify a long setup time with a long parts production run, which generates too much inventory. Instead, by reducing a setup to just a few seconds, it is a simple matter to run just a few parts, and then switch over the machine to some other needed part, which results in far less work-in-process inventory. Also, the department should focus on the highest possible levels of equipment preventive maintenance, since this keeps equipment from failing, which in turn keeps production manufacturing products in time for scheduled deliveries.

While all of these factors contribute to the manufacturing operations of a growing company, there are also several tasks that should be avoided. One is to steer clear of long production runs, especially those that exceed the maximum amount of product that is forecasted to be needed in the short run, since this will undoubtedly become excess inventory for some time and has the ancillary problems of an excessive cash investment in inventory, too much extra storage space, and the risk of product obsolescence, not to mention the extra cost of insuring the inventory. Another item to avoid is an excessive amount of work-in-process inventory, which happens when there is little coordination between the production of various work centers, which allows faster workstations to build more product than the downstream work centers can possibly handle. This results in the same problems just outlined—too much cash invested in inventory, extra storage, and the risk of obsolescence. Finally, the production staff should avoid an excessive amount of automation. Not only is automation expensive, but it is also difficult to reconfigure for new products, which is a key aspect of a short machine setup, short production run environment, as one finds in a facility that uses JIT concepts. A much better approach is to invest very little in much smaller, manually operated machines that have short setup intervals, and which are easily reconfigured for other work. In short, none of these practices have a place in a rapidly growing company and should be avoided.

The materials management function can contribute greatly to cash flows by tightly controlling both the timing and amount of cash flows into a company. For example, it can arrange with suppliers for them to make more frequent and smaller deliveries of parts to the company, so that it has to pay only for the lesser amounts received, and also eliminates the risk of never using some received parts. This tight scheduling can be accomplished by installing a material requirements planning (MRP) system, which combines the production schedule, on-hand inventory balances, and BOMs to arrive at the exact dates when parts should arrive from a supplier, as well as the exact quantities needed. This approach can be enhanced by giving suppliers electronic access to the MRP system, so that they can see the requirements for themselves. There are also several tasks to avoid, since they worsen cash flows. One is to spend extra amounts on inventory by using economic order quantities and safety stocks, which tend to result in excessive amounts of raw materials on hand. The department should also avoid a year-end physical inventory count, because this is far too infrequent an interval at which to review inventory accuracy. Instead, there should be a continual cycle counting program in place that counts small portions of the inventory every day and results in the investigation and resolution of any problems related to inaccurate inventory quantities. By attaining a much higher level of inventory accuracy, the materials management staff can rely on its inventory figures when ordering more parts and can dispense with any extra safety stock, which would otherwise cover parts that were missing from the inventory. When managed properly, these changes can result in enormous cash savings.

The sales and marketing departments are less concerned with cash flow and more concerned with monitoring the progress of sales growth. One such task is to periodically review unit sales and the average sale price for each product, to see if there is a gradual dropoff in sales. If so, the marketing staff must query customers regarding product changes that will spur sales and then communicate this information to the engineering staff, in order to create the next generation of products. Also, the marketing staff should closely monitor the activity and products of competitors and constantly reevaluate the company's position in relation to them, so that strategic changes can be made by the senior management team that will improve the company's sales in relation to them. The compensation package given to the sales staff should be heavily weighted in favor of commissions, so that it will have a large incentive to further increase sales to higher levels. The sales and marketing staffs should also avoid sales of specialized products, or sales to niche customers, because these types of sales will generally require much more staffing to create special products or to service customers and will not result in large or continuing sales gains. The best way to generate strong revenue growth is by concentrating on the center of the market for a product, not on expensive niches that will result only in higher costs and a much slower rate of sales growth.

Summary

After the preceding discussion of issues related to rapid growth, it is evident that a company must treat growth as not only an opportunity but also a dangerous problem. It requires a complete restructuring of the management team, the levels in the organization at which decisions are made, and an intense attention to cash flow, not to mention a possible change of ownership, or at least a sharing of control with new investors. For all these reasons, it is perhaps understandable why so many companies succumb to the allure of rapid growth without considering the changes that must occur at the same time. The specific alterations recommended in this chapter will help a corporation's owners and managers make the right decisions that will lead to a larger and more profitable organization.

Index

261